THE QUIET ART

A Doctor's Anthology

COMPILED BY

Dr. ROBERT COOPE

Scire potestates herbarum usumque medendi
Maluit et mutas agitare inglorius artes.

*It was his part to learn the powers of medicines and
the practice of healing, and careless of fame, to
exercise that quiet art.* VIRGIL, *Aeneid* XII, 396–7

E. & S. LIVINGSTONE LTD.
EDINBURGH & LONDON
1952

"For the honour of the profession, to continue in mutual love and affection among themselves, without which neither the dignity of the profession can be preserved, nor yet particular men receive that benefit by their admission into the profession which else they might expect, ever remembering that *Concordiâ res parvae crescunt, discordiâ magnae dilabuntur.*"

—extending William Harvey's directions to the Fellows and Members of the Royal College of Physicians to the whole profession.

Reprinted by the University of Alabama School of Medicine, University of Alabama at Birmingham, Birmingham, Alabama 35294, with permission from Longmans Publishing Group, Edinburgh, U.K., 1987. Printed in 1988.

Pictured on the cover is Tinsley R. Harrison, M.D. (1900–1978), Professor and Chairman of the Department of Medicine and Acting Dean of the University of Alabama School of Medicine, University of Alabama at Birmingham.

PRINTED IN GREAT BRITAIN

Light the lamps up, Lamplighter,
The people are in the street—
  Without a light
  They have no sight
And where will they plant their feet ?
Some will tread in the gutter,
And some in the mud—oh dear!
Light the lamps up, Lamplighter,
Because the night is here.

Light the candles, Grandmother,
The children are going to bed—
  Without a wick
  They'll stumble and stick,
And where will they lay their head ?
Some will lie on the staircase,
And some in the hearth—oh dear!
Light the candles, Grandmother,
Because the night is here.

Light the stars up, Gabriel,
The cherubs are out to fly—
  If heaven is blind
  How will they find
Their way across the sky?
Some will splash in the Milky Way,
Or bump on the moon—oh dear!
Light the stars up, Gabriel,
Because the night is here.

        ELEANOR FARJEON

ACKNOWLEDGMENTS

The author gratefully acknowledges his indebtedness to the following for the use of material from their publications:

Edward Arnold and Co.:
Sir Arthur Hurst, *A Twentieth-Century Physician*

A. and C. Black Ltd.:
Karl Pearson, *The Grammar of Science*

Blackwell Scientific Publications Ltd.:
R. H. Major, *Classic Descriptions of Disease*

The Syndics of the Cambridge University Press:
F. L. Lucas, *George Crabbe: an Anthology*
George Sampson, *Seven Essays*
C. H. Sorley, *Marlborough and Other Poems*

Constable and Co. Ltd.:
Sir H. H. Bashford ("Peter Harding, M.D."), *The Corner of Harley Street*
George Meredith, *Beauchamp's Career*
Cecil Woodham-Smith, *Florence Nightingale*

The Countryman

Peter Davies Ltd.:
Elizabeth Taylor, *At Mrs. Lippincote's*

J. M. Dent and Sons Ltd. (and A. P. Watt and Son):
Reginald L. Hine, *Confessions of an Uncommon Attorney*
Florence Converse, *The House of Prayer*

Victor Gollancz Ltd.:
Maude Royden, *A Threefold Cord*

Hamish Hamilton Ltd.:
H. Hesketh Pearson, *The Smith of Smiths*

Wm. Heinemann Ltd.:
John Galsworthy, *Poems*
Bernard Martin, *John Newton: a biography*

Wm. Heinemann Ltd. and Alfred A. Knopf, Inc., New York:
D. H. Lawrence, *Pansies*

Paul B. Hoeber, New York:
  W. C. Alvarez, *Nervousness, Indigestion and Pain*
Michael Joseph Ltd.:
  Eleanor Farjeon, *Silver-sand and Snow*
J. B. Lippincott Company, Philadelphia:
  Thorkild Rovsing, *Clinical Lectures on Abdominal Surgery*
Longmans, Green and Co. Ltd.:
  Dean Inge, *The Gate of Life*
Macmillan and Co. Ltd.:
  Christopher Hassall, *Poems*
  Sir Thomas Lewis, *Diseases of the Heart*
  C. G. Montefiore, *Aspects of Judaism*
  Confessio Medici
Macmillan and Co. Ltd. (and A. P. Watt and Son):
  Rudyard Kipling, "A Doctor's Work," from *A Book of Words*
The Mitre Press:
  Anna Bunston de Bary, *Under a Wiltshire Apple Tree*
The New Statesman and Nation
Oxford University Press (Clarendon Press):
  Sir Henry Cohen, *The Nature, Method and Purpose of Diagnosis*
  Sir James Learmonth, *The Contribution of Surgery to Preventive Medicine*
  Dr. Charles Singer, *The Legacy of Greece*
W. B. Saunders Co., Philadelphia:
  John Chalmers Da Costa, *Selected Papers and Speeches*
The Society of Authors and the Public Trustee:
  George Bernard Shaw, *The Doctor's Dilemma*
  John Masefield, *Philip the King*
  The Times; The Sunday Times; and to the following medical journals:
  Annals of the Royal College of Surgeons of England, British Journal of Tuberculosis, British Medical Journal, Bulletin of the Johns Hopkins Hospital, Edinburgh Medical Journal, Journal of the American Medical Association, Lancet, Liverpool Medico-Chirurgical Journal, Medical Press, and Practitioner.

  My most grateful thanks are due also to Mrs. George Bambridge, Mrs. Anna Bunston de Bary, Miss Eleanor Farjeon, Mr. Christopher

Hassall, the Very Rev. W. R. Inge, Miss Kathleen E. Innes, Mrs. Frieda Lawrence, the Executors of Dr. Harvey Cushing, the Executors of Sir Thomas Lewis, Mr. F. L. Lucas, Sir Desmond MacCarthy, Lord Macmillan, Professor John Macmurray, Dr. John Masefield, O.M., the Trustees of Claude G. Montefiore, the Hon. Harold Nicolson, the literary Executor of Sir Wm. Osler, Mr. H. Hesketh Pearson, the Trustees of Sir Michael Sadler, Mrs. Grace Sampson, Mrs. Cecil Woodham-Smith;

Dr. W. C. Alvarez, Dr. Hugh Barber, Mr. Norman R. Barrett, Sir H. H. Bashford, Dr. H. C. Cameron, Sir Henry Cohen, Dr. Terence East, Lord Horder, Dr. Clifford Hoyle, Sir Robert Hutchison, Sir Arthur Keith, Dr. W. N. Leak, Sir James Learmonth, Sir Heneage Ogilvie, Dr. Maurice Shaw, Dr. Charles Singer and Dr. F. M. R. Walshe.

If by inadvertence I have failed to make proper acknowledgment where it is due, I ask for forgiveness, and that I may be informed.

I am grateful to the Harveian Librarian of the Royal College of Physicians for the loan of the print from which the frontispiece is made.

My sincere thanks are due to my friend Dr. Gerard Sanderson who has given me much help and encouragement; and to Dr. John Robertson who has read through the proofs.

My wife has had a large share in the making of this book, especially in the final choosing of material, and as "a sorter out and placer of the principal matters contained therein."

To the publishers, and especially to Mr. Charles Macmillan and Mr. James Parker, I offer my thanks for the advice, the judgment, the care and the limitless trouble which they bring to bear to help an author and make a worthily produced book.

R. C.

LIVERPOOL, 1952

FOREWORD

An anthology, according to the dictionary, is a collection of flowers, and the flower-collector enjoys both the pleasures of familiarity and the excitements of new discovery, both of which are to be found in this volume. The reader may well wonder at the rich and varied flora of medical thought. Is there anything comparable in the other professions? Do lawyers in their quieter moments write on the human aspects of torts, or architects turn from calculations of window space and sunlight to compose hymns to Apollo? I do not know. But doctors may justly feel proud of their profession's contributions to literature. Of course the material of their art is uniquely interesting. The doctor occupies a seat in the front row of the stalls of the human drama, and is constantly watching, and even intervening in, the tragedies, comedies and tragi-comedies which form the raw material of the literary art. If the doctor is to be capable of his work, he must be a man of feeling; and if he is to do his work, his feelings must often in great measure be denied expression. Perhaps this is partly the reason why doctors express themselves in writing, but it does not explain why they so often express themselves well, nor why so many authors, some among the most distinguished, have come to the writing of poetry, plays or novels by way of medicine. Whatever the explanation, we may all be grateful that so many doctors, whether they have achieved literary fame or not, have written clearly and gracefully, humorously and movingly about the fundamentals of life and of their profession. Sir William Osler once wrote: "A rare and precious gift is the Art of Detachment by which a man may so separate himself from a life-long environment as to take a panoramic view of the conditions under which he has lived and moved: it frees him from Plato's den long enough to see the realities as they are, the shadows as they appear. Could a physician attain to such an art he would find in the state of his profession a theme calling as well for the exercise of the highest faculties of description and imagination as for the deepest philosophic insight." Here, then, is the quiet art of medicine illuminated by the quiet art of the anthologist.

W. RUSSELL BRAIN,
President of the Royal

LONDON, 1952
College of Physicians.

DEDICATION

THIS volume is dedicated to the memory of Tinsley R. Harrison, M.D., founder and first editor-in-chief of the text now known as *Harrison's Principles of Internal Medicine.* Harrison, a disciple of William Osler, epitomized the characteristics exemplified in the aphorisms of this volume. He contributes the following paragraphs, the first and the last paragraphs from the Introduction of his *Principles,* reprinted here from the first edition:

> No greater opportunity, responsibility, or obligation can fall to the lot of a human being than to become a physician. In the care of the suffering he needs technical skill, scientific knowledge, and human understanding. He who uses these with courage, with humility, and with wisdom will provide a unique service for his fellow man, and will build an enduring edifice of character within himself. The physician should ask of his destiny no more than this; he should be content with no less.

> ***

> Tact, sympathy, and understanding are expected of the physician, for the patient is no mere collection of symptoms, signs, disordered functions, damaged organs, and disturbed emotions. He is human, fearful, and hopeful, seeking relief, help, and reassurance. To the physician, as to the anthropologist, nothing human is strange or repulsive. The misanthrope may become a smart diagnostician of organic disease, but he can scarcely hope to succeed as a physician. The true physician has a Shakespearean breadth of interest in the wise and the foolish, the proud and the humble, the stoic hero and the whining rogue. He cares for people.

INTRODUCTION

DURING the 1940s and 1950s there was in London, England, a fine practitioner of medicine, a physician who was an excellent general physician as well as an expert in lung diseases and their diagnosis and management. This was Robert Coope, M.D. He was sought out as a preceptor by young physicians throughout the world who wished to emulate his excellence in helping people and dealing with their diseases, particularly pulmonary maladies.

The reasons, in part, for Dr. Coope's excellence are evident in this anthology of quotations which he compiled and published in 1952. The selections speak for themselves; the choices speak volumes of the basic decency, old British civility, and essential goodwill toward all human beings which were characteristic of this physician.

Surely, good attitudes toward patients, toward medicine, and toward life in general are the beginning of good medicine. It is for this reason that the University of Alabama School of Medicine, UAB, is republishing this volume, in the hope that others may also profit from it.

JAMES A. PITTMAN, JR., *M.D., Dean*
University of Alabama School of Medicine
University of Alabama at Birmingham
Birmingham, Alabama

CONTENTS

I

THE SCIENCE AND THE ART

A

The Very Nature of Things

In the beginning was the Logos *; the Logos was with God and the Logos was God. He was with God in the beginning. Through him all things came into being, nothing that exists came into being apart from him. In him was Life, and this life was the Light of men. The Light shines on in the darkness, and the darkness has never conquered it.

* (That is, the Word, the creative self-revealing of God.)

The Gospel of St. John, i. 1-5.

We Need the Enquiring Mind

Some things I have said of which I am not altogether confident. But that we shall be better and braver and less helpless if we think that we ought to enquire, than we should have been if we indulged in the idle fancy that there was no knowledge and no use in seeking to know what we do not know—that is a theme upon which I am ready to fight, in word and deed, to the utmost of my power.

PLATO
Meno.

The Inner Light

Blessed is he who carries within himself a God, an ideal of beauty, and who obeys it; ideal of art, ideal of science, ideal of the fatherland, ideal of the virtues of the Gospel, for therein lie the springs of great thoughts and great actions; they all reflect light from the Infinite.

PASTEUR, *in his reception oration at the Académie des Sciences.*

[3]

The Scope of Science

Now this is the peculiarity of scientific method, that when once it has become a habit of mind, that mind converts *all* facts whatsoever into science. The field of science is unlimited; its solid contents are endless, every group of natural phenomena, every phase of social life, every stage of past or present development is material for science. *The unity of all science consists alone in its method, not in its material.* The man who classifies facts of any kind whatever, who sees their mutual relation and describes their sequence, is applying the scientific method and is a man of science. The facts may belong to the past history of mankind, to the social statistics of our great cities, to the atmosphere of the most distant stars, to the digestive organs of a worm, or to the life of a scarcely visible bacillus. It is not the facts themselves which form science, but the method in which they are dealt with. The material of science is co-extensive with the whole physical universe, not only that universe as it now exists, but with its past history and the past history of all life therein. When every fact, every present or past phenomenon of that universe, every phase of present or past life therein, has been examined, classified, and co-ordinated with the rest, then the mission of science will be completed. What is this but saying that the task of science can never end till man ceases to be, till history is no longer made, and development itself ceases?

KARL PEARSON
The Grammar of Science, 1911.

Beware of Prejudices

If I set out to prove something, I am no real scientist—I have to learn to follow where the facts lead me—I have to learn to whip my prejudices.

SPALLANZANI, 1729-1799.

[4]

Ever Widening Fields

Every great advance of science opens our eyes to facts which we have failed before to observe, and makes new demands on our powers of interpretation. This extension of the material of science into regions where our great-grandfathers could see nothing at all, or where they would have declared human knowledge impossible, is one of the most remarkable features of modern progress. Where they interpreted the motion of the planets of our own system, we discuss the chemical constitution of stars, many of which did not exist for them, for their telescopes could not reach them. Where they discovered the circulation of the blood, we see the physical conflict of living poisons within the blood, whose battles would have been absurdities for them.

KARL PEARSON
The Grammar of Science, 1911.

Have the Mind for Truth

My determination is not to remain stubbornly with my ideas, but I will leave them and go over to others as soon as I am shown no other purpose than to place truth before my eyes so far as it is in my power to embrace it: and to use the little talent I have received to draw the world away from its old heathenish superstitions, and to go over to the truth and to stick to it. . . .

Almost all of the courses they teach there (i.e. The University of Leyden) are for the purpose of getting money through knowledge, or for gaining the respect of the world by showing how learned you are, and these things have nothing to do with discovering the things that are buried from our eyes. . . . A man has always to be busy with his thoughts if anything is to be accomplished.

LEEUWENHOEK, 1632-1723.

[5]

Of the Study of Natural History

There is yet another way in which natural history may, I am convinced, take a profound hold upon practical life—and that is, by its influence over our finer feelings, as the greatest of all sources of that pleasure which is derivable from beauty. I do not pretend that natural-history knowledge, as such, can increase our sense of the beautiful in natural objects. I do not suppose that the dead soul of Peter Bell, of whom the great poet of nature says:—

> A primrose by a river's brim
> A yellow primrose was to him,
> And it was nothing more—

would have been a whit roused from its apathy by the information that the primrose is a Dicotyledonous Exogen, with a monopetalous corolla and central placentation. But I advocate natural-history knowledge from this point of view, because it would lead us to *seek* the beauties of natural objects, instead of trusting to chance to force them on our attention. To a person not instructed in natural history, his country or sea side stroll is a walk through a gallery filled with wonderful works of art, nine-tenths of which have their faces turned to the wall. Teach him something of natural history, and you place in his hands a catalogue of those which are worth turning round.

T. H. HUXLEY, 1825-1895
Science and Education.

Where Truth is to be Found

I know that truth lies in the facts, and not in the mind that judges of them, and that the less I introduce what is merely my own into the deductions I make from them, the more certain I shall be of approaching the truth.
ROUSSEAU

The Secret of Knowledge

The only means, therefore, of guarding ourselves from being misled by false theories, or by the mis-application of those that are true, is to gain a thorough acquaintance with both, whether originating in learning or in ignorance. I say *thorough*, for the philosophic poet in stating the beneficial influence of a liberal education on the practice of life, does not say simply *didicisse*,

> ingenuas didicisse fideliter artes,
> Emollit mores nec sinit esse feros—OVID.

but *FIDELITER didicisse*; that is thoroughly, and in good earnest. In a word, we should strive to attain, if possible, that only criterion of substantial and profound knowledge, that of *knowing how little we know*. This is the only cure for overweening vanity and self-conceit, and the only standard by which we ought to measure our own intellectual attainments and those of others.

Sir GILBERT BLANE
Elements of Medical Logick, 1825.

Impediments to Knowledge

Too great dependence on authority;
Allowing too great weight to custom;
Fear of offending the vulgar;
The affectation of concealing ignorance by the display of a specious appearance of knowledge.

ROGER BACON, 1214-1294.

The Pain of a New Idea

Sooner or later—insensibly, unconsciously—the iron yoke of conformity is upon our necks: and in our minds, as in our bodies, the force of habit becomes irresistible. From our teachers and associates, from our reading, from the social atmosphere about us, we catch the beliefs of the day, and they become ingrained—part of our nature. For most of us this happens in the haphazard process we call education, and it goes on just as long as we retain any mental receptivity. It was never better expressed than in the famous lines that occurred to Henry Sidgwick in his sleep:

We think so because all other people think so;
Or because—or because—after all, we do think so;
Or because we were told so, and think we must think so:
Or because we once thought so, and think we still think so;
Or because, having thought so, we think we will think so.

. . . Walter Bagehot tells us that the pain of a new idea is one of the greatest pains to human nature. "It is, as people say, so upsetting; it makes you think that, after all, your favourite notions may be wrong, your firmest beliefs ill-founded; it is certain that till now there was no place allotted in your mind to the new and startling inhabitant; and now that it has conquered an entrance, you do not at once see which of your old ideas it will not turn out, with which of them it can be reconciled, and with which it is at essential enmity."

OSLER
Harveian Oration, 1906.

Useful Knowledge

The knowledge which a man can use is the only real knowledge, the only knowledge which has life and growth in it, and converts itself into practical power. The rest hangs like dust about the brain, or dries like raindrops off the stones.

FROUDE

Of Pseudo-Science

I shall begin, my friends, with the definition of a *Pseudo-Science*. A Pseudo-science consists of a *nomenclature*, with a self-adjusting arrangement, by which all positive evidence, or such as favours its doctrines, is admitted, and all negative evidence, or such as tells against it, is excluded. It is invariably connected with some lucrative practical application. Its professors and practitioners are usually shrewd people; they are very serious with the public, but wink and laugh a good deal among themselves. The believing multitude consists of women of both sexes, feeble-minded inquirers, poetical optimists, people who always get cheated in buying horses, philanthropists who insist on hurrying up the millennium, and others of this class, with here and there a clergyman, less frequently a lawyer, very rarely a physician, and almost never a horse-jockey or a member of the detective police. . . .

A Pseudo-science does not necessarily consist wholly of lies. It may contain many truths, and even valuable ones. . . . The practitioners of the Pseudo-sciences know that common minds, after they have been baited with a real fact or two, will jump at the merest rag of a lie, or even at the bare hook. When we have one fact found us, we are very apt to supply the next out of our own imagination.

OLIVER WENDELL HOLMES, 1809-1894
The Professor at the Breakfast-Table.

[9]

Truth of Speaking

Be assured of this, most excellent Crito, that to use words in an improper sense is not only a bad thing in itself, but it generates a bad habit in the soul.

PLATO

One Form of Untruth

There is something worse than deliberate lying, and that is the habit of gratuitous assertion; of saying, not what we know to be untrue, but what we do not know to be true. Nine-tenths of our untruthfulness is of this sort; and it is fostered by the credulity or the indifference of our hearers.

Father GEORGE TYRRELL

Of the Use of Theory

Without theory, practice is but routine born of habit. Theory alone can bring forth and develop the spirit of invention. It is to you specially that it will belong not to share the opinion of those narrow minds who disdain everything in science which has not an immediate application. You know Faraday's charming saying. He was witnessing the first demonstration of a purely scientific discovery, and people round him said, "But what is the use of it?" Faraday answered them, "What is the use of a new-born child?" . . . A theoretical discovery has but the merits of its existence. It awakens hope, and that is all. But let it be cultivated, let it grow, and you will see what it will become.

PASTEUR, to his pupils at Lille

Muddle

Depend upon it, the nation that is muddled in its prose is muddled in its thoughts. The people who cannot say what they mean are people who do not know what they mean. Never were people so muddled as we of this nation are today. And why? Because we muddle our minds with words of imprecise meaning—the word "education" being one of the most imprecise of all. Beware of all abstract nouns in politics. Liberty, Equality and Fraternity danced the Carmagnole round the guillotine.

GEORGE SAMPSON
Seven Essays.

Indecision Leads Nowhere

If you go buzzing about between right and wrong, vibrating and fluctuating, you come out nowhere; but if you are absolutely and thoroughly and persistently wrong, you must some of these days have the extreme good fortune of knocking your head against a fact, and that sets you all right again.

T. H. HUXLEY
Science and Education.

The Way

This is the way of salvation—to look thoroughly into everything, and see what it really is, alike in matter and in cause; with your whole heart to do what is just and say what is true; and one thing more, to find life's fruition in heaping good on good so close that not a chink is left between.

MARCUS AURELIUS

Of Study

Naturall Abilities, are like Naturall Plants, that need Proyning by Study: and Studies themselves, doe give forth Directions too much at large, except they be bounded in by Experience. . . . Reade not to Contradict, and Confute; Nor to Beleeve and Take for granted; Nor to find Talke and Discourse; But to weigh and Consider. Some Bookes are to be Tasted, Others to be Swallowed, and Some Few to be Chewed and Digested; That is, some Bookes are to be read onely in Parts; Others to be read but not Curiously; And some few to be read wholly, and with Diligence and Attention. Some Bookes also may be read by Deputy, and Extracts made of them by Others: But that would be onely in the lesse important Arguments, and the Meaner Sort of Bookes; else distilled Bookes, are like common distilled Waters, Flashy Things. Reading maketh a Full Man; Conference a Ready Man; and Writing an Exact Man. And therefore, if a Man Write little, he had need have a Great Memory; if he Conferre little, he had need have a Present Wit; and if he Reade little, he had need have much Cunning, to seem to know that, he doth not.

FRANCIS BACON, 1561-1626
Essayes.

Four Sorts of Readers

An old writer says that there are four sorts of readers: "Sponges which attract all without distinguishing; Howreglasses which receive and powre out as fast; Bagges which only retain the dregges of the spices and let the wine escape, and Sives which retaine the best onely."

OSLER
Books and Men, 1901.

Experience

That is the worst of learning from experience; it takes too long. Often it takes a lifetime. "Experience," said Sainte-Beuve, "is like the pole-star; it only guides a man in the evening, and rises when he is going to rest."

REGINALD L. HINE
Confessions of an Uncommon Attorney.

Harvey and the Experimental Method

Not so much really in the demonstration of the method—the *Inventum mirabile* sought for by Descartes, the *Novum Organum* for Bacon—lies the true merit of Harvey's work. While Bacon was thinking, Harvey was acting; and before Descartes had left his happy school at La Flêche, Harvey was using *la nouvelle méthode*; and it is in this way that the *de Motu Cordis* marks the break of the modern spirit with the old traditions. No longer were men to rest content with careful observations and with accurate descriptions; no longer were men to be content with finely spun theories and dreams, which "serve as a common subterfuge of ignorance"; but here for the first time a great physiological problem was approached from the experimental side by a man with a modern scientific mind, who could weigh evidence, and not go beyond it, and who had the sense to let the conclusions emerge naturally but firmly from the observations. To the age of the hearer, in which men had heard, and heard only, had succeeded the age of the eye, in which men had seen and had been content only to see. But at last came the age of the hand—the thinking, devising, planning hand; the hand as an instrument of the mind, now reintroduced into the world in a modest little monograph of seventy-two pages, from which we may date the beginning of experimental medicine.

OSLER
Harveian Oration, 1906.

[13]

The Background of Medical Practice

... they are as a sleep: in the morning they are like grass which groweth up. In the morning it flourisheth and groweth up; in the evening it is cut down, and withereth. We spend our years as a tale that is told.

The years of our life are three score years and ten; or if by reason of strength they are four score years, yet is their strength then labour and sorrow: for it is soon cut off, and we are gone.

Psalm xc.

Eryximachus Speaks of Medicine

My art further informs me that the double love is not merely an affection of the soul of man towards the fair, or towards anything, but is to be found in the bodies of all animals and in productions of the earth, and I may say all that is; such is the conclusion which I seem to have gathered from my own art of medicine, whence I learn how great and wonderful and universal is the deity of love, whose empire extends over all things, divine as well as human.

So too in the body the good and healthy elements are to be indulged and the elements of disease are not to be indulged, but discouraged. And this is what the physician has to do, and in this the art of medicine consists: for medicine may be regarded generally as the knowledge of the loves and desires of the body, and how to satisfy them or not; and the best physician is he who is able to separate fair love from foul, or to convert one into the other; and he who knows how to eradicate and how to implant love, whichever is required, and can reconcile the most hostile elements in the constitution and make them loving friends, is a skilful practitioner.

PLATO
Symposium.

Rare Satisfaction

I should never have been happy in any profession that did not call forth the highest intellectual strain, and yet keep me in good warm contact, with my neighbours. There is nothing like the medical profession for that: one can have the exclusive scientific life that touches the distance, and befriend the old fogies in the parish too.

GEORGE ELIOT
Middlemarch.

Foundations

Whoever is to acquire a competent knowledge of medicine ought to be possessed of the following advantages: a natural disposition for instruction: a favourable position for study: early tuition: love of labour: leisure. First of all, a natural talent is required; for when Nature leads the way to what is most excellent, instruction in the art takes place, which the student must try to appropriate to himself by reflection, becoming an early pupil in a place well adapted for instruction. He must also bring to the task a love of labour and perseverance, so that the instruction taking root may bring forth proper and abundant fruits.

HIPPOCRATES
The Law.

The Greek Influence on Medicine

The critical sense and sceptical attitude of the Hippocratic school laid the foundation of modern medicine on broad lines, and we owe to it: *first*, the emancipation of medicine from the shackles of priestcraft and of caste; *secondly*, the conception of medicine as an art based on accurate observation, and as a science, an integral part of the science of man and of nature; *thirdly*, the high moral ideals, expressed in that "most memorable of human documents" (Gomperz), the Hippocratic oath; and *fourthly*, the conception and realization of medicine as the profession of a cultivated gentleman.

OSLER
Chauvinism in Medicine, 1902.

The Art of Medicine

Medicine—however much it develops—must always remain an "applied science," and one differing from all the rest in that the application is to man himself. Were there no sick persons there would be no need for Medicine, either the Science or the Art. So long as there are, both will be necessary. The application of its Science, to be of value, must be made in such a way that it will produce the maximum of relief to the sick man. ·This calls for certain qualities in the practising physician which differ entirely from anything required in the practice of the other applied sciences. Herein lies the Art of Medicine. The need for it is as great today as it ever was, or ever will be, so long as human sickness continues.

Sir ARTHUR HALL
Practitioner, 1941.

Medicine as Understanding

Most men form an exaggerated estimate of the powers of medicine, founded on the common acceptation of the name, that medicine is the art of curing diseases. That this is a false definition is evident from the fact that many diseases are incurable, and that one such disease must at last happen to every living man. A far more just definition would be that medicine is the art of understanding diseases, and of curing or relieving them when possible. Under this acceptation our science would, at least, be exonerated from reproach, and would stand on a basis capable of supporting a reasonable and durable system for the amelioration of human maladies.

Dr. Jacob Bigelow
Nature in Disease, 1852.

Theory and Practice

Sagacity in practice, the art of applying so much of larger theory as may be useful and of combining it readily with current empirical rules, a good memory for symptoms, and a quickness in giving what painters call true values to each symptom of a group are qualities partly innate, partly learned in the wards, partly in the world. But even these great qualities are of less effect if associated, as too often they are, with unverified premises and random speculations.

Another source of fallacy is the vicious circle of illusions which consists on the one hand of believing what we see, and on the other in seeing what we believe. If we believe that a necklace of coral fades with the health of the wearer, we shall see what we look for; if we see a child after taking paeony root get the better of an epilepsy, we may forget that this prescription of Oribasius always contains with the root an active purgative. When we read in the Life of Charles Wesley that a plaster of egg and brimstone on brown paper

B   [17]

cured his sickness, we may omit to observe that, as Dr. Paris tells us, he also followed the prescriptions of Dr. Fothergill, which was country air, rest, asses' milk, and horse exercise.

Another besetting fallacy lies in what has been called, from the days of Aristotle, equivocal terms. The meaning of words is not precisely defined, and we, as we argue, slip unconsciously out of one meaning into another. . . .

Finally let me point out one more danger—that is the danger not only of attaching too high and too permanent an estimate to our empirical laws or maxims within their own sphere, and of forgetting how relative and transitory their values are, but also of carrying them beyond our own sphere, and applying to other orders of phenomena rules which, even within their own order, have to be used with caution and reserve. Yet this error is committed daily, even by medical men. Medical men, let us say, formulate a maxim that insanity, speaking generally, is apt to be hereditary; or that phthisis pulmonalis is infectious—both useful maxims, and indicative of much truth, but far enough from scientific laws. Yet with these imperfect and rather ricketty instruments some medical men do not hesitate to invade the sphere of jurisprudence, or the sphere of ethics and civil order, and to order people about in courts of law or in contracts of marriage, forgetting that the very difficulty of using general laws on any large scale, even in medicine itself, and that the difficulties of particular cases which arise under the incursions of the causes of secondary and tertiary perturbations, and which are embarrassing enough in medicine, are still more embarrassing in the more complex orders of ethics and of society.

CLIFFORD ALLBUTT
Theory and Practice
B.M.J., 1897.

Integrated Medicine

The harm done by the attempt to separate our examination of the patient's function into two sharply differentiated portions and to assign one portion to the individual known as the laboratory man and the other portion to some one called a "clinician"—the harm, I say, done by this attempt consists in part in a loss of essential facts in the transfer from one man to another. For such data are not readily transferable like coin without loss of value. Few can interpret the results of blood examination, or urinary examination, unless they are constantly making such examinations themselves. Indeed the attempt so to interpret them is almost as hopeless as the attempt to convey satisfactorily to another what one feels in the palpation of the abdomen. Laboratory facts are *personal* facts as much as the results of palpation, and they are almost as difficult to convey to a second person. Moreover, our interpretation of the crude data obtained by our senses is apt to be a very faulty one if we attempt, as a so-called laboratory man often has to do, to make this interpretation wholly uninfluenced by the clinical aspects of the case. Those best trained in microscopical and chemical analysis are coming more and more to feel unwilling to hand over to another man any hard and fast conclusions based upon the isolated facts in his possession. More and more we are finding that the men who examine scrapings or fragments of a tumour want to see the case in the wards and get possession of all the facts ascertainable, just as the clinician is more and more unwilling to accept a report from the laboratory without seeing the specimens himself.

R. C. CABOT
The Ideal of Accuracy in Clinical Work
Boston M. and S. Journal, 1904.

Essential Knowledge

To know the natural progress of diseases is to know more than the half of medicine. . . . There is a sufficiently easy method of acquiring this knowledge so important to the practitioner. Observe the practice of many physicians; do not implicitly believe the mere assertion of your master; be something better than servile learners; go forth yourselves to see and compare! . . . Knowing, henceforth, the physiognomy of the disease when allowed to run its own course, you can, without risk of error, estimate the value of the different medications which have been employed. You will discover which remedies have done no harm, and which have notably curtailed the duration of the disease; and thus for the future you will have a standard by which to measure the value of the medicines which you see employed to counteract the malady in question. What you have done in respect of one disease, you will be able to do in respect of many; and by proceeding in this way you will be able, on sure data, to pass judgment on the treatment pursued by your masters.

TROUSSEAU, 1801–1867
Lectures on Clinical Medicine.

The Imperfect Instrument

Let it, however, be remarked that practical medicine takes this shape from its own necessity, as things are. Our knowledge is incomplete. But such as it is, we must use it; and the first condition of using it safely or profitably is to know that it is incomplete. An imperfect instrument is in our hands, and we cannot trust it simply and entirely. It needs some art and management in the handling; but these must not be too much, lest they hurt the fair play of our instrument, imperfect as it is.

Dr. PETER MERE LATHAM
Lectures on Clinical Medicine, 1836.

[20]

Experience

In rare instances the practising physician becomes the creative scientist. His imagination conceives of an hypothesis, based on frequent, accurate, well controlled observation. This hypothesis is put repeatedly and rigidly to the test by carefully planned, albeit simple, experiments on the human being. Many of the experiments of Harvey, the discovery of Jenner, and the work of Laennec were of this type. But science, for most men, does not progress much beyond the descriptive method, and knowledge is sought and obtained by accurate observations of natural phenomena, recorded with meticulous care, collected, compared, controlled by further observations, subjected to critical analysis, and finally brought to a conclusion uninfluenced by desire or theory. This method results in what is commonly known as *experience*, a word interpreted in the Middle Ages as signifying experiment, and used to-day by the French to describe experiment. But at times, in experience and during experiments, desire warps judgment, and the love of a theory leads to disaster.

WARFIELD T. LONGCOPE
Methods and Medicine
Bull. Johns Hopkins Hospital, 1932.

Nature's Aptitude

Homoeopaths, very unintentionally and unwittingly, I admit, came opportunely to teach us to recognise the inherent forces of the living economy. Their successes, based with precision upon cures which they attribute to themselves, but which belong exclusively to nature, have been useful lessons to us. They have taught us to rely a little less on ourselves and a little more on the wonderful aptitude of the tissues and apparatus which constitute the animal machine.

TROUSSEAU
Lectures on Clinical Medicine.

[21]

Beware of Dogma

There is nothing in which a young practitioner should be more on his guard, than being misled by the sweeping dogmas of schools, and the indiscriminate practices of sects, or of favourite practitioners. This evil may be conceived to grow up in the mind of a tyro, in the following manner. Let him at his outsetting, either at a school of physick, or in witnessing the practice of some private practitioner, meet with one or two impressive and imposing cases, terminating happily under a particular treatment; this will attach him undeviatingly to the like kind of practice for the remainder of his life, unless his mind should be duly prepared by the caution here inculcated. In a typhous fever, for instance, it may be the lot of one practitioner, while serving his noviciate, to have witnessed, either under his own care, or that of some respected instructor, one or two striking cures, from an exhibition of strong cordials; another has witnessed life saved, as he believed, by well timed and free evacuation from the bowels; to a third, it has occurred to see beneficial effects from general or local blood-letting; to a fourth it has occurred to see one or two cases which being left in a great measure to themselves, have, by the salutary effects of kind nature, been conducted to a safe termination. Now, each of these having from his limited opportunities of observation, imbibed a persuasion, that his own method is universally applicable, is guided by it as the rule of his future practice. Nothing seems more clear to a comprehensive mind, than that they are all four right, in so far as relates to their respective class of cases; and that they are all wrong in regard to the general principles of practice.

Sir GILBERT BLANE
Elements of Medical Logick, 1825.

[22]

Specialism

Medicine as a whole is too vast for the grasp of any one individual. Specialism is inevitable, and having accepted it we must examine its limitations. The essential and inescapable one is that a specialist is expert for one purpose only. A specialist alone can be supremely efficient, and the earlier he devotes himself to a particular branch of study, the smaller that branch, and the more single-minded the devotion with which he studies it, the more efficient will he be in that branch and that alone. But disease is no specialist. Patients do not consult us because certain organs are affected, but because they feel ill. They come with symptoms, and the earlier and therefore the more curable their malady is, the more vague will those symptoms be, the more difficult the elucidation of their cause, the greater the need, in the first place, of a general investigation by one whose daily practice covers the whole of disease.

Sir HENEAGE OGILVIE, Lancet, 1948.

Science and the Art

Take care not to fancy that you are physicians as soon as you have mastered scientific facts; they only afford to your understandings an opportunity of bringing forth fruit, and of elevating you to the high position of a man of art. . . . Do not, therefore, fancy yourselves physicians because you have acquired the habit of applying to the diagnosis of diseases the ingenious proceedings by which science has become enriched since the beginning of this century. The admirable diagnostic methods—auscultation and percussion—given by Laennec to the public for the general good, and of which no one is allowed to be ignorant, are in our hands what the telescope and the magnifying-glass are in the hands of the astronomer and the naturalist—instruments intermediary between external objects and the mind; but a magnifying-glass will no more make a Tournefort or a Galileo, than a stethoscope will make a Sydenham or a Torti.

TROUSSEAU, Lectures on Clinical Medicine.

Always a Learner

Each one of us, however old, is still an undergraduate in the school of experience. When a man thinks he has graduated, he becomes a public menace.

JOHN CHALMERS DA COSTA
Selected Papers and Speeches, 1931.

Humility of Mind

Start out with the conviction that absolute truth is hard to reach in matters relating to our fellow creatures, healthy or diseased, that slips in observation are inevitable even with the best trained faculties, that errors in judgment must occur in the practice of an art which consists largely in balancing probabilities;—start, I say, with this attitude of mind, and mistakes will be acknowledged and regretted; but instead of a slow process of self-deception, with ever increasing inability to recognize truth, you will draw from your errors the very lessons which may enable you to avoid their repetition.

And for the sake of what it brings, this grace of humility is a precious gift. When to the sessions of sweet silent thought you summon up the remembrance of your imperfections, the faults of your brothers will seem less grievous, and, in the quaint language of Sir Thomas Browne, you will "allow one eye for what is laudable in them." The wrangling and unseemly disputes which have too often disgraced our profession arise, in a great majority of cases, on the one hand, from this morbid sensitiveness to the confession of error, and, on the other, from a lack of brotherly consideration, and a convenient forgetfulness of our own failings.

OSLER
Teacher and Student, 1892.

[24]

Our Experience

We physicians had need to be a self-confronting and a self-reproving race; for we must be ready, without fear or favour, to call in question our own experience, and to judge it justly; to confirm it, to repeal it, to reverse it, to set up the new against the old, and again to reinstate the old and give it preponderance over the new.

Belief, opinion, truth! When we cast up the sum of a long experience, by which of these names shall we call it? Its subject is one of the worthiest, even nothing less than the life and well-being of man. Let it then be spoken of in the handsomest terms it deserves. And it is hard if there be not something in the results of experience that is worth the name of truth. But then it is an infirmity of men, finding a fragment of truth, to take it for the whole truth; or, intent upon what may well pass for truth now and for a few years to come, to account it the truth which stands fast for ever and ever. We must be cautious, then, not to deceive ourselves, or take the truth there is in the practice of medicine for what it is not. If what can be apprehended by fragments but not completely, if what lasts safe and sure and trustworthy for times and seasons but not for ever, can be called truth, this is the truth, which is vouchsafed us to know and to use in the practice of medicine, and this only. And we must make the best of it, and be content.

Dr. PETER MERE LATHAM
Lectures on Clinical Medicine, 1836.

The Fleshly Tabernacle

It is our proud office to attend the fleshly tabernacle of the immortal spirit, and our path, if rightly followed, will be guided by truth unfettered and love unfeigned. In the pursuit of this noble and holy calling I wish you all God-speed.

LISTER, *Graduation Address at Edinburgh.*

[25]

Physick a Hard Taskmaster

It will be seen, how vain all acquired knowledge is, without practical habits; for in the liberal, as well as the mechanical arts, expertness can be obtained only by frequent and long-continued exercise of actual labour; and it is by a happy and appropriate figure, that those who are skilled in languages, painting, eloquence, physick, or the common business of life, are said in Latin, *callere*, whence *callidus*, words derived from *callus*, that is, a horny substance formed on the hands of mechanical artisans, by long and unremitting labour. . . . So true is it, according to the common apophthegm, that *practice only can make perfect*, or that *Jack of all trades is good at none;* or let us draw a more dignified illustration from Cicero, who says:

Nec MEDICI, nec imperatores, nec oratores, quamvis artis praecepta perceperint, quidquam magna laude dignum, sine usu et exercitatione consequi possunt.

Was it not clearly the intention of the author, in placing physicians here in the foremost rank, to intimate, that, of all professions, the most severe discipline of practice and experience, was required in physick?

Sir GILBERT BLANE
Elements of Medical Logick, 1825.

Our Task

To wrest from nature the secrets which have perplexed philosophers in all ages, to track to their sources the causes of disease, to correlate the vast stores of knowledge, that they may be quickly available for the prevention and cure of disease—these are our ambitions. To carefully observe the phenomena of life in all its phases, normal and perverted, to make perfect that most difficult of all the arts, the art of observation, to call to aid the science of experimentation, to cultivate the reasoning faculty, so as to be able to know the true from the false—these are our methods. To prevent disease, to relieve suffering and to heal the sick—this is our work. The profession in truth is a sort of guild or brotherhood, any member of which can take up his calling in any part of the world and find brethren whose language and methods and whose aims are identical with his own.

OSLER
Chauvinism in Medicine, 1902.

Theory and Practice

If we reason from individual cases only, as too often we do, we may possibly score even some small successes, but such successes may be in conflict with larger and more important ends. We may lower arterial pressure or we may bring down temperature, but we may be as far or even farther away from the cure of the patient. We shall rather visit continually the sources of the contemplative man and, entering into his researches, select from his store certain parts of his science, parts adapted to our ends, and arrange them for practical purposes; they may include our empirical aphorisms or they may dissipate them, or indeed they may conflict with them; if they conflict with them we shall hold our own imperfect maxims a little longer and meanwhile take the problem back again and again to the laboratory, which is good for the contemplative man, as it brings him down to mother earth where, like Antaeus, he will renew his strength. Thus between theory and practice we shall put together some intermediate truths, which will serve us for a while; and though we are certainly doomed but too often to fail *ex ignorantia*—that is for lack of fuller enlightenment —we shall not fail *ignoranter*—that is for lack of teachableness. Blindfold we often are; headstrong we need not be.

CLIFFORD ALLBUTT
Theory and Practice, B.M.J., 1897.

The Art and Craft

Medicine requires not only the intellectual cultivation of
a science, but the patience and practical skill of an art. At
the bedside we must be animated by the feeling of faithful
artisans, of men whose object and duty is practical work;
for when the art of Medicine is needed by the suffering and
the dying it is no question of mere theoretical knowledge
and extraneous acquirement. But skill in the commonest
art is not to be attained without much practice, far less in
the complicated and difficult art of healing, where every case
presents some peculiarities. To practise it successfully, we
must have made our home at the bedside, and, if I may say so,
have lived with disease, observing it in all its forms and changes.

Sir WILLIAM GULL
The Study of Medicine, 1855.

" *A Little less science and a little more art, gentlemen* "

I am well aware that in these days, when a student must be
converted into a physiologist, a physicist, a chemist, a bio-
logist, a pharmacologist, and an electrician, there is no time
to make a physician of him. That consummation can only
come after he has gone out in the world of sickness and
suffering, unless indeed his mind is so bemused, his instincts
so dulled, his sympathy so blunted by the long process of
education in those sciences, that he is forever excluded from
the art of medicine, which was to Hippocrates "the art" of
all arts. In that case he is destined for the laboratory, the
professor's chair, or the consultant's office. What would
have happened to Sydenham had he been put through this
machinery is a problem in infinity which no human intelligence is competent to solve.

Sir ANDREW MACPHAIL
The Source of Modern Medicine, B.M.J., 1933.

II

STUDENTS ALL

We Owe a Debt

A Rabbi was once passing through a field where he saw a very old man planting an oak-tree. "Why are you planting that tree?" said he. "You surely do not expect to live long enough to see the acorn growing up into an oak-tree?"

"Ah," replied the old man, "my ancestors planted trees not for themselves, but for us, in order that we might enjoy their shade or their fruit. I am doing likewise for those who will come after me."

The Talmud.

The Price of Teaching

It was his firm conviction that the teacher had failed in his intentions if at the end of his discourse he was not mentally exhilarated and physically exhausted.

Said of Noah Morris: late Professor of Therapeutics, University of Glasgow
Lancet, 1947.

Let the Froth Settle

Those of us who have the duty of training the rising generation of doctors must not inseminate the virgin minds of the young with the tares of our own fads. It is for this reason that it is easily possible for teaching to be too "up-to-date." It is always well, before handing the cup of knowledge to the young, to wait until the froth has settled.

Sir ROBERT HUTCHISON
Fashions and Fads in Medicine
B.M.J., 1925.

An Exacting Vocation

To you affectionate children will look for the welfare of their parents; to you the anxious parent will turn for the rescue of his child; and on you the fond husband will depend for all that is dear to him in the hour of danger; to you, perhaps, may be confided the lives of numerous men led to the field of battle, or marched, through unwholesome countries; to you the health and efficiency of crews destined to long and perilous navigation may be entrusted; on you the public eye is to be bent in days of plague and pestilence, for who shall now say that from such visitations even our happy climate may be free? And under all these circumstances you must be ready to give an account of what has been done, not only to those who are eagerly collected around you, but to a much more troublesome inquirer within, who will accompany you to the retirement of your closet, and with its inquisitorial voice not only ask you whether you have done your best upon the present occasion, but whether from the time you commenced your professional studies you used your utmost exertions to acquire that knowledge, which would fit you for the discharge of your duties; for it is this consciousness alone which can enable you to lie down with comfort when harassed by the occasional unsuccessful issue even of your best endeavours.

RICHARD BRIGHT
Introductory Lecture to Students, 1832.

A Good Teacher

And though this payneful pastor now be dead,
He conscious is that here his flock he fed
In wolsome pastures, adding to his name
A crown of glory which outways all fame.

Memorial in Little Burstead Church, Essex.

The Teacher Speaks to the Student

It would be useless for me at this time to go into a more detailed development of the system of instruction I wish you to follow. It will be gradually unfolded as you advance, and may be modified by circumstances; and in all your intercourse with me I wish you to look upon me merely as an older student than yourself, who, having trod the same path, has a greater knowledge of its difficulties, and pleasures, and dangers; who will be proud to be your guide, and glory in inspiring you with an ardent love of the profession you have chosen. I feel deeply impressed with the belief that your character and talents are such as eminently to qualify you for attaining distinction as a medical philosopher and gaining the respect and affection of those among your fellow men who may require your professional services. I will not conceal from you that there is much before you to make even a strong resolution waver. You must toil for years to fit you for the guardianship of the health and lives of men; and yet again you must toil long and diligently, to reap the reward of your labour. But if you have a spark of benevolence in your heart; if you have that only ambition which is not vice—to excel others in doing good; if you think that the gratitude and the affection of those you may relieve from sickness is a sufficient recompense for much self-denial and self-sacrifice, then you will not be disappointed. You will be richly repaid for your days of labour and your nights of watching; you will learn to cultivate a spirit of charity towards others, and of justice toward yourself, which will make your station in life respectable and your social and domestic relations hallowed by the light of an unbroken peace.

Dr. ALFRED STILLÉ, quoted by
Osler in *An Alabama Student.*

The Teacher at the Bedside

Whenever I have entered my wards, I have been accustomed to regard myself in no other light than that of one who presides over a great solemnity, and is engaged so to manage all its circumstances that they shall produce their appropriate impression upon the mind of the spectators. You are those spectators; and the solemnity you witness has many scenes and several actors, and one main subject runs through the whole. The scenes are the diversified incidents of many diseases; the actors are the sick themselves, and those who minister to them—the nurse, the physician, and the physician's attendants; and the great subject of the whole is the life of human beings consigned to our hands for a time and used and treated according to our pleasure, and always for purposes of good. This life is by all means to be saved; its diseases by all means to be alleviated or cured; and the arts and methods of saving, and curing, and alleviating are to be so displayed, that the benefit and blessings of individuals may be multiplied infinitely.

But how multiplied infinitely? Even through you. Recollect you are the spectators; I am but the actor. For this is a case in which the spectator's place is a thousand times more important than that of the prime agent, if the measure of things be calculated by the result. My business is with the few individual patients before me; and whatever good or whatever evil I do, would be strictly limited to them, but for your presence. Yes, you are there to take note of the errors into which I may fall, that you may avoid them, and so restrict the mischief within its present sphere; and you are there to take note, also, of the good which I may do, and learn the method of doing it, and make it your own, and carry it abroad with you, that it may bear fruit an hundred-fold, and be multiplied among all mankind.

Dr. PETER MERE LATHAM
Lectures on Clinical Medicine, 1836.

[34]

For a Teacher's Comfort

What you have done by counsel, inspiration and warning, by words from the pulpit and in confidential talk, and by your writing, will be like radium, animating for years and years the individuals and the institutions which have come within the range of your compassion.

> MICHAEL SADLER to Hudson Shaw, quoted in
> *A Threefold Cord* by Maude Royden.

The Noble Heritage

Whilst you are young, and while you make your first essay in arms, let your fields be the hospitals and the clinics; when your knowledge has increased, let the hospitals and clinics continue to be your fields of industry after you have acquired all the scientific knowledge which we exact from you at the probationary examinations. By pursuing this plan, you will attain expertness in the practice of your art, knowing what science teaches, and having the power within yourselves of originating; then, also, will you begin that priesthood which will honour you, and to which you will do honour; then, too, will begin the life of sacrifice; in which your days and nights will be the patrimony of your patients. You must resign yourselves to sow in devotion that which you must often reap in ingratitude; you must renounce the sweet pleasures of the family, and that repose so grateful after the fatigue of laborious occupations; you must know how to confront loathsomeness, mortifications of spirit, and dangers; you must not retreat before the menaces of death, for death achieved amid the perils of your profession will cause your names to be pronounced with respect.

> TROUSSEAU
> *Lectures on Clinical Medicine.*

Ward Round

I'm ill. I send for Symmachus; he's here,
An hundred pupils following in the rear:
All feel my pulse, with hands as cold as snow;
I had no fever then—I have it now.   MARTIAL
                                        Epigrams.

To the Bedside!

This very question of medical education was put to
Sydenham by Hans Sloane, who afterwards achieved the
highest professional and social honours, and is yet remembered as the founder of the British Museum. The young
man modestly suggested that he might take a course in
anatomy and botany. "This is all very fine," said Sydenham;
"but it won't do. Anatomy, botany—nonsense, sir. I know
an old woman in Covent Garden who understands botany
better; and as for anatomy, my butcher can dissect a joint
full as well. No, young man; all this is stuff: you must go
to the bedside; it is there alone you can learn disease."
Rather than go abroad to study botany, he recommended
this earnest seeker to drown himself in a pond that was
commonly used for that purpose. The frightful thing is that
he may have been right.   Sir ANDREW MACPHAIL
                              The Source of Modern Medicine
                              B.M.J., 1933.

Teachers and Students

Medical students naturally have faith in their instructors,
turning to them for truth, and taking what they may chose
to give them: babies in knowledge, not yet able to tell the
breast from the bottle, pumping away for the milk of truth
at all that offers, were it nothing better than a professor's
shrivelled forefinger.   OLIVER WENDELL HOLMES

Specialisation

To decry specialisation in education is to misinterpret the purpose of education. The true aim of the teacher must be to impart an appreciation of method and not a knowledge of facts. This is far more readily achieved by concentrating the student's attention on a small range of phenomena, than by leading him in rapid and superficial survey over wide fields of knowledge. Personally I have no recollection of at least 90 per cent. of the *facts* that were taught to me at school, but the notions of *method* which I derived from my instructor in Greek Grammar (the contents of which I have long forgotten), remained in my mind as the really valuable part of my school equipment for life.

KARL PEARSON
The Grammar of Science, 1911.

Initiation

I had been a medical student for four years before I knew what I wanted to do with my life, and my course was determined when, in 1907, I opened the pages of Sherrington's *Integrative Action of the Nervous System*, which Professor Bayliss had put into my hands. This book, one that later ages will, I firmly believe, acclaim as one of the few imperishable books in the history of medicine and physiology, was no part of the curriculum of the day; and had my teachers taken the narrow view that nothing should be imparted to me but what was of proven value to the general practitioner as he was then known, I might well have missed one of the most exciting mental experiences of my life.

Dr. F. M. R. WALSHE
Teachers of Medicine
Lancet, 1947.

[37]

Medicine a Craft

It is in medicine as in the piloting of a ship—rules may be laid down, principles expounded, charts exhibited; but when a man has made himself master of all these, he will often find his ship among breakers and quicksands, and must at last have recourse to his own craft and courage.

Dr. JOHN BROWN
Horae Subsecivae, 1861.

The Art of Medicine

Medicine in practice is not yet so scientific as many like to pretend; indeed it is only comparatively recently that it has even been described as a science. Hippocrates always spoke of the "art" and the same is true of all medical writers after him down to quite modern times. But one of the tendencies of the present day is to exaggerate the "scientificness" (if I may use the term) of medicine. . . . In the first place it is responsible for the cluttering up of the medical curriculum with all sorts of "ologies", most of which the student forgets as soon as he has passed the examination in them. This leads to much waste of time for, as Samuel Butler said with much truth, "a physician's physiology has much the same relation to his power of healing as a cleric's divinity has to his power of influencing conduct. . . ."

Last and worst, the ultra-scientific outlook leads to a wrong attitude towards our work at the bedside. As Sir Auckland Geddes has put it, "so many come to the sickroom thinking of themselves as men of science fighting disease and not as healers with a little knowledge helping nature to get a sick man well."

Sir ROBERT HUTCHISON
Practitioner, 1937.

[38]

The Essence of a Teaching Hospital

I know of no better definition of the objects of a teaching hospital than Nathaniel Faxon's—"to advance knowledge, to train doctors, and to set an example of practice."

Dr. F. M. R. WALSHE
Teachers of Medicine
Lancet, 1947.

Lazy Student

'Tis the voice of a sluggard; I heard him complain—
"You have waked me too soon; I must slumber again."
As the door on its hinges, so he on his bed
Turns his sides and his shoulders, and his heavy head.

"A little more sleep and a little more slumber"—
Thus he wastes half his days, and his hours without number;
And when he gets up, he sits folding his hands,
Or walks about saunt'ring, or trifling he stands.

I passed by his garden, and saw the wild briar,
The thorn and the thistle grow broader and higher;
The clothes that hang on him are turning to rags;
And his money still wastes till he starves or he begs.

I made him a visit, still hoping to find
That he took better care for improving his mind;
He told me his dreams, talked of eating and drinking,
But he scarce reads his Bible, and never loves thinking.

Said I then to my heart: "Here's a lesson for me;
That man's but a picture of what I might be;
But thanks to my friends for their care in my breeding,
Who taught me betimes to love working and reading."

Dr. ISAAC WATTS
Divine Songs for Children, 1715.

[39]

An Uphill Road

You must always be students, learning and unlearning till your life's end, and if, gentlemen, you are not prepared to follow your profession in this spirit, I implore you to leave its ranks and betake yourself to some third-class trade.

LISTER

Time, Gentlemen, Please!

One thing seems certain—if we taught more and examined less, our students would learn more. If we add anything further to the medical curriculum let it be spare time.

Grains and Scruples
Lancet, 1938.

Let Your Yea be Yea

There is the story of the examiner who was a bully. He became quite impatient with an Indian candidate and bawled at him: "Answer me, yes or no. Has this patient got mitral stenosis?" The gentleman from the East edged up to him until he was quite close and gave the answer in a whisper "Perhaps."

As the Examiner sees it
Lancet, 1947.

Misconception

In answer to a question on the treatment of haematemesis, countless candidates said that the patient must be given oyster soup. This was traced to a lecturer lately imported from Glasgow who had told them to give the patient "ice to suck."

As the Examiner sees it
Lancet, 1947.

Too Much Busyness

In these modern days hardly any one of us, whatever his position, can devote enough time to meditation, and if the stress continues this will be a bad thing for preventive medicine and for surgery. Many of the relatively obvious problems of preventive medicine and of surgery have been solved or are in process of solution, and at least an equal number of problems might emerge from the meditations upon these of those practising the two branches of the medical profession. Nowadays, only too often Higher Authority (spelled with capital letters) errs in mistaking busyness for business, a strategic error crystallised in the phrase by Lord Asquith. John Hunter meditated much and long over his own problems, and if they are to lead effective lives graduates who are the intake into preventive medicine must do so also. This poses an arresting educational problem, and its solution must begin in the elementary and secondary schools. My own experience tempts me to declare that on the whole there is no vainer appeal to many of the present-day taught than the appeal to "think it out."

Sir James Learmonth
The Contribution of Surgery to Preventive Medicine, 1951.

Of Examinations—A Warning to Teachers

Epictetus cleverly illustrates this very system and its fruits: "As if sheep, after they have been feeding, should present their shepherds with the very grass itself which they had cropped and swallowed, to show how much they had eaten, instead of concocting it into wool and milk."

Dr. John Brown
Horae Subsecivae, 1861.

Too Much Reading

Excessive reading may be a form of laziness. . . . If you spend most of your time in reading, you are likely to be left not only with no time for the more important occupations of observing and thinking, but with no mind wherewith to do these essential things.

LORD HORDER
The Vocation of Medicine
Lancet, 1948.

A Book for Students

Read Don Quixote; it is a very good book—I read it still.

SYDENHAM, 1624–1689.

Busy in His Craft

A leech should be always busy about things belonging to his craft. He must either be talking about it or studying it or be writing or praying, for the use of books brings a doctor a good reputation because it is both noticed by others and he himself becomes wiser thereby.

A leech ought also to have well cut clothes, dressing soberly and not like a clown or a poet. He ought too to have clean hands and well shaped nails which should not be black or filthy. He should behave himself courteously at a lord's dining table and he should not offend the guests who are sitting near him either in words or deeds. He should hear many things but speak little; the wise man says "it is better to use the ears than the tongue."

Master JOHN ARDERNE, 1307–1380
On the behaviour of a leech.

The Important " Final "

The Oxford Final Schools and the Day of Judgment are two examinations, not one.

Sir WALTER RALEIGH
(*Sometime Professor of Poetry at Oxford.*)

Advice to Young Men

"Free yourself," said Cobbett in his *Advice to Young Men*, "from the slavery of tea and coffee and other slopkettle." Doctors tell their patients never to touch it: yet it is odd, wherever I go into a coffee-house, they themselves are coming in, or sending in, for coffee. It was a doctor, I remember, who passed on to me the oriental secret of the making of coffee, that it must be "as sweet as love, as black as sin, and as hot as hell."

REGINALD L. HINE
Confessions of an Uncommon Attorney.

On some Uses of a Library

The testy librarian of tradition, miserly of his treasures, nearsightedly buried in his latest acquisitions, impatient of interruption, is an extinct species. And if such persons really ever existed beyond the pages of fiction it would be charitable of us to ascribe their traits to the absent-mindedness that a most exacting task is prone to engender. You have doubtless heard how late one afternoon the college librarian started home with a friend, and finding it raining went back to get his umbrella. As he did not reappear he was sought out and found confusedly looking for the object under " U " in the library catalogue.

HARVEY CUSHING
Consecratio Medici, 1929.

[43]

Of Medical Societies

The functions of a medical society are social and educational, and of these the first is undoubtedly more important, because it leads naturally to the second. . . . Unity and friendship among the doctors of a district is most easily brought about by the pleasant and free intercourse which a well-conducted dinner meeting of a medical society provides.

Here they can meet without the formality that attends the gatherings of a larger body, the majority of whose members are strangers to each other. Here they can discuss medical matters to their hearts' content without the guilty feeling, always present at a non-medical party, that they are talking shop. Here the practitioner can repair after he has finished his busy surgery, and meet his friends and rivals over a cocktail or a glass of sherry, and, equally important, his wife can meet the wives of his friends and rivals. Misunderstandings are cleared up, suspicions and animosities melt away. If a good dinner follows, and an easy address and discussion, many men will find themselves ready to get up and speak freely of their experiences without that reserve and uneasy boastfulness that affects them at many of the formal discussions. Thus the social functions of a medical society lead naturally to the educational, because without a broad and tolerant frame of mind a doctor cannot be educated or, rather, he cannot educate himself.

Sir HENEAGE OGILVIE
Lancet, 1946.

Of Doctors' Meetings

The Hunterian Society at first used taverns as its meeting-places. It was claimed by the Council over 100 years ago: "They have met as members of the medical family should meet, with truth and science for their objects and honesty and charity for their guides."

The Times, Feb. 13, 1948.

It Might be Said of Some Speakers!

Hee was (indeed) honest, and of an open, and free nature: had an excellent *Phantsie*; brave notions, and gentle expressions: wherein he flow'd with that facility that sometime it was necessary he should be stop'd.

BEN JONSON speaks of Shakespeare
Discoveries, 1641.

One of the Talkers

Gratiano speaks an infinite deal of nothing, more than any man in all Venice. His reasons are as two grains of wheat, hid in two bushels of chaff: you shall seek all day ere you find them; and when you have found them, they are not worth the search.

SHAKESPEARE
Merchant of Venice, i. 1. 114

Of Speaking at Meetings

"Blessed is the man," says George Eliot, "who, having nothing to say, abstains from giving us wordy evidence of the fact, from calling us to look through a heap of millet seed in order to be sure that there is no pearl in it." One of the greatest men of last century, who was largely responsible for remodelling the map of Europe, was said to have a magnificent faculty of silence in ten languages.

Dr. G. A. GIBSON
The Uses of Debate, 1904.

Be Good Natured

Our Fallibility and the Shortness of our Knowledge should make us peaceable and gentle: because I *may* be mistaken, I *must* not be dogmatical and confident, peremptory and imperious.

> BENJAMIN WHICHCOTE, 1609-1683
> One of the Cambridge neo-platonists.

A Word to Controversialists

An *Asse* was so hardy once, as to fall a mopping and braying at a *Lyon*. The Lyon began at first to shew his teeth, and to stomach the affront; but upon second thought; Well! (says he) *Jeer on, and be an Asse still.* Take notice only by the way, that 'tis the baseness of your character that has sav'd your carcass.

> AESOP
> *Fables*
> Translated by Sir Roger L'Estrange.

III

VIGNETTES

The man is Hippocrates himself. Of the actual details of his life we know next to nothing. His period of greatest activity falls about 400 B.C. He seems to have led a wandering life. Born of a long line of physicians in the island of Cos, he exerted his activities in Thrace, Abdera, Delos, the Propontis (Cyzicus), Thasos, Thessaly (notably at Larissa and Meliboea), Athens and elsewhere, dying at Larissa in extreme old age about the year 377 B.C. He had many pupils, among whom were his two sons Thessalos and Drakon, who also undertook journeys, his son-in-law Polybus, of whose works a fragment has been preserved for us by Aristotle, together with three other Coans bearing the names Apollonius, Dexippus, and Praxagoras. This is practically all we know of him with certainty. But though his glimpse is very dim and distant, yet we cannot exaggerate the influence on the course of medicine and the value for physicians of all time of the traditional picture that was early formed of him and that may indeed well be drawn again from the works bearing his name. In beauty and dignity that figure is beyond praise. Perhaps gaining in stateliness what he loses in clearness, Hippocrates will ever remain the type of the perfect physician. Learned, observant, humane, with a profound reverence for the claims of his patients, but an overmastering desire that his experience shall benefit others, orderly and calm, disturbed only by anxiety to record his knowledge for the use of his brother physicians and for the relief of suffering, grave, thoughtful and reticent, pure of mind and master of his passions, this is no overdrawn picture of the Father of Medicine as he appeared to his contemporaries and successors. It is a figure of character and virtue which has had an ethical value to medical men of all ages comparable only to the influence exerted on their followers by the founders of the great religions. If one needed a maxim to place on the statue of Hippocrates, none could be found better than that from the book Παραγγελίαι, Precepts:

ἢν γὰρ παρῇ φιλανθρωπίη, πάρεστι καὶ φιλοτεχνίη,

"Where the love of man is, there also is love of the Art."

Dr. CHARLES SINGER
The Legacy of Greece, 1921
(both excerpts).

A Great Man's Opportunities

Hippocrates himself practised only in little towns, not one of which was of itself sufficient to support a single physician. Most of his observations were made in Thessaly and Thrace; and he names only small cities. Galen somewhere says that the smallest quarter in Rome contained more inhabitants than the largest town in which Hippocrates practised. It is, therefore, not the great number of patients, but the capacity for deriving all the possible information from each particular case, which tends to form the experienced physician.

ZIMMERMANN
A Treatise on Experience in Physic, 1782.

The Hippocratic Physicians

The physicians of the Hippocratic school remain, for the most part, patient observers of fact, sceptical of the marvellous and unverifiable, hesitating to theorise beyond the data, yet eager always to generalise from actual experience; calm, faithful, effective servants of the sick.

Dr. CHARLES SINGER
The Legacy of Greece.

Galen's Portrait of a Quack

Galen has given us the portrait of every quack in that which he has drawn of Thessalus, who lived in the reign of Nero. His father, says he, was a workman, who tried in vain to give some idea of what was great and beautiful. Without the least tincture of letters or philosophy, Thessalus took it into his head to begin as a physician; and according to his own gross way of thinking he really was so. Soon, however, he perceived that he was deficient in many points of knowledge, and in the qualities which are capable of leading on a man with credit in his profession. He still preserved the tone, the manners, and the language of the man of trade; and it was by no means difficult to distinguish in him the carder of wool. He began, therefore, to win upon his patients, not by prescribing them remedies properly adapted to the circumstances of their case, but by flattering their hopes and sacrificing to their vanity. Notwithstanding the natural severity of his temper, he knew how to mould himself occasionally to the will of his patients, when he saw that his low complaisance would turn to good account. But with all his suppleness to those whose favour he had gained or wished to gain, he shewed the greatest impudence and temerity towards all regular practitioners; and he had no sooner succeeded at Rome by this meanness than he exclaimed without reserve against all physicians; and even went so far as to assert that he himself was the only one who deserved that title. He was not less injurious to the dead than to the living; and even took pleasure in reviling the memory of Hippocrates.

Dr. Zimmermann
A Treatise on Experience in Physic, 1782.

With us ther was a DOCTOUR OF PHISIK;
In all this world ne was ther noon hym lik,
To speke of phisik and of surgerye;
For he was grounded in astronomye.
He kepte his pacient a ful greet deel
In houres, by his magyk natureel.
Wel koude he fortunen the ascendent
Of his ymages for his pacient.
He knew the cause of everich maladye,
Were it of hoot, or cold, or moyste, or drye,
And where they engendred and of what humour;
He was a verray parfit praktisour.
The cause y-knowe and of his harm the roote,
Anon he yaf the sike man his boote.
Ful redy hadde he his apothecaries
To sende him drogges and his letuaries,
For ech of hem made oother for to wynne,
Hir friendshipe nas nat newe to bigynne.
Wel knew he the olde Esculapius
And Deyscorides, and eek Rufus,
Olde Ypocras, Haly and Galyen,
Serapion, Razis and Avycen,
Averrois, Damascien and Constantyn,
Bernard and Gatesden and Gilbertyn.
Of his diete mesurable was he,
For it was of no superfluitee,
But of greet norissyng and digestible.
His studie was but litel on the Bible.
In sangwyn and in pers he clad was al,
Lyned with taffata and with sendal.

And yet he was but esy of dispence,
He kepte that he wan in pestilence.
For gold in phisik is a cordial,
Therfore he lovede gold in special.

GEOFFREY CHAUCER
Prologue to the Canterbury Tales.

Mark Akenside

Mark Akenside (1721-1770) brought out *The Pleasures of the Imagination* in his twenty-third year and then, becoming a haughty physician to St. Thomas' and Christ's hospitals, and Goulstonian and Croonian Lecturer at the Royal College of Physicians, remained to all intents poetically dumb until the year of his death.

SIR HUMPHRY ROLLESTON
Poetry and Physic
B.M.J., 1925.

Lines on the Tomb of Dr. Jenner

Within this tomb hath found a resting-place
The great physician of the human race—
Immortal JENNER!—Whose gigantic mind
Brought life and health to more than half mankind.
Let rescued infancy his worth proclaim,
And lisp out blessings on his honour'd name;
And radiant beauty drop one grateful tear,
For beauty's truest friend lies buried here.

Professional Anecdotes, 1825.

Harvey the Man

Love of truth, reverence and charity, with some tincture of imagination and humour, these were the chief features of Harvey's personality; but to complete the picture we must add moral courage—which Michael Foster said is an essential part of the scientific character—patience and reflectiveness. It must have required much moral courage to attack the Galenic stronghold, and it is no wonder that Zachary Wood apostrophised him as "Truly a bold man, indeed, O disturber of the Quiet of Physicians! O Seditious Citizen of the Physical Commonwealth!" His patience was shown not only in the carrying out of his investigations, but in his reluctance to make them public. He always bided his time. He was like Darwin, who waited 29 years for the results of a single experiment, and all of whose work on evolution was published after he was 50. In his slowness to publish he resembled other great men of his time, and the next century, Galileo, Newton, Bacon, Cavendish and Gauss. How different from us today with our "preliminary notes" and disputes as to precedence in discovery! Lastly, he was a reflective philosopher. Like Hunter his delight was to think. We are told that he would withdraw himself to the leads of his house in town, or to caves in his garden in the country, in order to indulge in contemplation. Surely in this also he has a lesson for our unreflective time.

Sir ROBERT HUTCHISON
Harveian Oration, 1931.

A Crack-brained Fellow?

I hear that you have a great good opinion of Dr. Harvey. He is a most excellent anatomist, but in the practicke part of his Physicke, I conceive him to be mutch, many times, governed by his Phantasye.

LORD CONWAY, *in a letter to his daughter*, 1640.

[54]

A New World

I must trouble you with a date, 1685, the year in which Charles II died. That reign marks the watershed between the mediaeval and the modern world; between the mass and the individual; between authority and experience; between books and experiment. From that summit the spring of modern medicine burst forth. It was in reality a new world. The Royal Society had been founded; the circulation of the blood had been proven; the Cartesian method had been disclosed; the universal law of gravity and the laws of planetary motion had just been announced. Logarithms, electricity, magnetism, chemistry, were words coming into common use. Up to that time the authority in science was Aristotle; in philosophy, Thomas; in medicine, Galen. All three had organised and synthesised the existing knowledge of their day. It was a useful task; but when life is too closely organised it begins to perish. The body of knowledge then becomes a burden, a tradition; it blinds men's eyes; it makes them incapable of observation or thought. It enslaves them; but suddenly, freedom asserts itself. Freedom too has perils, but they are less dangerous than the perils of slavery. One can now say what he likes, even in medicine, no matter how foolish; there will be plenty to contradict him.

There were reasons deeper still for the scientific renascence of the period under review. The divine right in science of Aristotle and the Greeks had passed; the divine right of kings in politics perished at the hand of Cromwell; the divine right of Galen in medicine came to an end with the appearance of Thomas Sydenham.

Sir ANDREW MACPHAIL
The Source of Modern Medicine
B.M.J., 1933.

Thomas Sydenham

Sydenham was a Roundhead trooper in the first phase of the Civil War and a captain in the second phase. It was not till comparatively late in life that he turned his mind to medicine. In the eyes of his contemporaries he was a rebel, and when political events forced him to another sphere of activity he remained a rebel—the "trooper turned physician" in Dr. Karcher's phrase. In that fact Dr. Karcher finds the explanation of Sydenham's devotion to the ascertainment of natural phenomena, and of his repugnance to the established order of medical science. It is remarkable that a Roundhead with a well-known record of activity in the Civil Wars rose so soon to distinction and lucrative practice in the early days of the Restoration; for there is no evidence that he suffered for his political opinions. His immunity must partly be ascribed to the intimate friendships he had formed at Oxford with some of the distinguished men of the time. Boyle and Locke were his close friends and he seems to have known most of the circle who composed the Royal Society. That Sydenham's military experiences contributed to the formation of his mature ideas is highly probable, but they were hardly the determining factor. It must not be forgotten that Sydenham was well educated—not indeed a scholar or learned in the sense that Willis or Lower, his contemporaries, were learned, but with a fine command of his own tongue. Some of his English writing, of which but little has come to us, is magnificent in natural eloquence and balanced rhythm. Moreover, he was an ardent student and admirer of Bacon and Hippocrates, and also, apparently, of Don Quixote. He, too, found tilting at windmills a congenial occupation, and was a far more skilful performer than the Don. . . . It is strange that Sydenham never mentioned William Harvey and seems to have been unaware of the discovery of the capillary circulation by

Malpighi in 1661. But he stands in the direct line of progress in his appeal to facts. "Non fingendum aut excogitandum, sed inveniendum quid natura faciat aut ferat," the motto which he adopted from Francis Bacon for the title-page of his *Tractatus de Podagra et Hydrope*, expresses the same watchword as Hunter's advice to Jenner: "Do not think; try."

Lancet, *annotation*, 1940.

Sydenham

A hypochrondriac was advised by Sydenham to consult a physician in Inverness. The man proceeded on horseback; he could not find the doctor; he returned very angry but cured. "Nothing," said Sydenham, "so cherishes and strengthens the blood and spirits as riding a horse."

Sir ANDREW MACPHAIL
The Source of Modern Medicine
B.M.J., 1933.

Presence of Mind

A mendicant on London Bridge, while bolting a piece of meat in a hurry, was suffocated on the spot by a portion entering the glottis. A crowd was quickly collected. A resurrection-man rushed through them, burst into tears, and cried, oh, my brother! The sympathising spectators soon procured a hackney-coach, in which the resurrection-man quietly conveyed the corpse to a dissecting room, and pocketed the premium.

The Medico-Chirurgical Review, 1825.

Frère Jacques

His name was Jacques Beaulieu and he was born in the year 1651 in a hamlet called Etendonne. His parents were poor farmers and even as a boy he knew that he could never be satisfied with the squalor and ignorance of the peasants. At the age of 16 he had already made up his mind to seek out his fortune in the world, and to this end he had learned to read and write and had decided to be a surgeon. . . .

In the year 1690 he decided to change his mode of life; he altered his name to Frère Jacques and became a monk, but he did not join any of the recognised brotherhoods. His dress was distinctive and of his own design; he wore a hat instead of a cowl, and slippers upon his feet; his vows were devised by himself and arranged to suit his occupation. . . . At the age of 69 he returned to his own village; on the 7th December 1714, he died in the house of his friend Laurent Decart . . . A most singular man, to whom surgery owes a great deal. He is said to have operated upon 4500 patients for the stone, and another 2000 for hernia, in the short span of 19 years which covered his period as an active surgeon. . . . After Frère Jacques, Cheselden (1688-1752) and other famous surgeons trod the same ground in England and in Europe, and the light he lit guided them to perfection. But more than this, he showed courage and a dignified bearing in the face of powerful critics; in contrast to the custom of his time, he relied upon nature to heal the wounds he had made. He was calm and quiet when he operated, and he treated the poor and the humble to the utmost of his skill. His mistakes were not so much his own as those of the period in which he lived, and his contributions to knowledge were ahead of current beliefs. He gave to those who followed him an operation and an example of behaviour.

N. R. BARRETT
Ann. Roy. Coll. Surg. Eng., 1949.

Himself the Guinea Pig

Frustrated by the inconclusive evidence of clinical practice, John Hunter set to work upon a crucial experiment. He deliberately infected himself with venereal poison with a lancet, watched the early signs and symptoms, and then delayed treatment month after month that he might the better study the effects of the disease. Eventually, after three years close observation, he considered himself cured. As he tells the story there is no self-pity, no self-conceit, no expression of foolhardiness; it is just a plain unvarnished account, quietly recorded, of his search for the truth about a problem of infective disease which baffled him. Comment on this act of personal courage seems out of place. He postponed his marriage and waited until he was entirely free from signs and symptoms. We cannot guess what passed through his mind during those three years, all we know, in the light of modern research, is that he was certainly ignorant of the far-reaching results of venereal disease. Many of the facts were correctly observed, but the deductions were wrong and in the end the experiment cost Hunter his life. More than half a century elapsed before Ricord unravelled the problem of the separate entity of syphilis, but Hunter's work and personal sacrifice had not been in vain. He had tried to explain the sequence of signs and symptoms which had hitherto been largely obscured by secrecy and concealment; he had described with meticulous care the march of events in the primary infection, and one sign of this, the Hunterian chancre, still bears his name; and he had lifted the whole unsavoury subject out of the mire of quackery and made it a serious scientific study.

Dr. S. Roodhouse Gloyne
John Hunter.

John Hunter's Coronary Thrombosis

(i) In the spring of 1769, in his forty-first year, he had a regular fit of the gout, which returned the three following springs, but not in the fourth; and in the spring of 1773, having met with something which very forcibly affected his mind, he was attacked, at ten o'clock in the forenoon, with a pain in the stomach, about the pylorus: it was the sensation peculiar to those parts, and became so violent, that he tried change of position to procure ease; he sat down, then walked, laid himself down on the carpet, then upon chairs, but could find no relief. He took a spoonful of tincture of rhubarb with 30 drops of laudanum, without the smallest benefit. While he was walking about the room, he cast his eyes on the looking-glass, and observed his countenance to be pale, his lips white, giving the appearance of a dead man: this alarmed him, and led him to feel for his pulse; but he found none in either arm. He now thought his complaint serious. Several physicians of his acquaintance were then sent for: Dr. William Hunter, Sir George Baker, Dr. Huck Saunders, and Sir William Fordyce, all came, but could find no pulse; the pain still continued, and he found himself at times not breathing. Being afraid of death soon taking place if he did not breathe, he produced the voluntary act of breathing, by working his lungs by the power of the will; the sensitive principle, with all its effects on the machine, not being in the least affected by the complaint. In this state he continued for three quarters of an hour, in which time frequent attempts were made to feel the pulse, but in vain; however, at last, the pain lessened, and the pulse returned, although at first but faintly, and the involuntary breathing began to take place. While in this state, he took Madeira, brandy, ginger, etc., but did not believe them of any service, as the return of health was very gradual; in two hours he was perfectly recovered.

(ii) On the 16th of October 1793, when in his usual state of health, he went to St. George's Hospital, and meeting with some things which irritated his mind, and not being perfectly master of the circumstances, he withheld his sentiments; in which state of restraint he went into the next room, and turning round to Dr. Robinson, one of the physicians of the hospital, he gave a deep groan, and dropt down dead!

JOSEPH ADAMS
Memoirs of the Life and Doctrines of the late John Hunter, Esq., 1817.

John Hunter and the Body-snatchers

There was in London at that time an Irish giant (O'Brian) whose case interested Hunter a great deal, and as the man was in declining health he was anxious at his death to secure the skeleton. The giant, who was eight feet tall, became aware that he was of more than common interest to the doctors and that he was being kept under observation. He therefore left instructions that at his death his body should be watched night and day until a leaden coffin could be prepared and a burial at sea carried out. Hunter entered into secret arrangements with a group of body snatchers through the medium of one of his servants. The resurrection men evidently knew their man, and the price for the body went up by leaps and bounds from fifty to five hundred pounds. Hunter had to borrow the money but he procured his prize, which was surreptitiously carried to Earl's Court, where the skeleton was secretly prepared for his museum. After Hunter's death it found its way with the rest of his collection to the Royal College of Surgeons' Museum.

Dr. S. ROODHOUSE GLOYNE
John Hunter.

Boerhaave

Boerhaave lectured five hours a day; his hospital contained only twelve beds, but by Sydenham's method he made of it the medical centre of Europe.

Sir ANDREW MACPHAIL
The Source of Modern Medicine
B.M.J., 1933.

Parish Doctor

Anon, a figure enters, quaintly neat,
All pride and business, bustle and conceit;
With looks unalter'd by these scenes of woe,
With speed that, entering, speaks his haste to go,
He bids the gazing throng around him fly,
And carries fate and physic in his eye:
A potent quack, long versed in human ills,
Who first insults the victim whom he kills;
Whose murd'rous hand a drowsy Bench protect,
And whose most tender mercy is neglect.
Paid by the parish for attendance here,
He wears contempt upon his sapient sneer;
In haste he seeks the bed where misery lies,
Impatience mark'd in his averted eyes;
And, some habitual queries hurried o'er,
Without reply, he rushes on the door.

GEORGE CRABBE
The Village, 1783.

Fulness of Life

I divided my life into three parts: in the first I learned my profession, in the second I taught it, in the third I enjoy it.

Sir BLAND SUTTON

John Abernethy

The lecture room was the grand theatre upon which Mr. Abernethy displayed; there, indeed, he "shone eccentric, like a comet's blaze" and there he would indulge his disposition and propensities to an extent which occasioned the pupils frequently to regard it as an exhibition, and call it an "Abernethy at Home." His mode of entering the lecture room was often irresistibly droll—his hands buried deep in his breeches-pockets, his body bent slouchingly forward, blowing or whistling, his eyes twinkling beneath their arches, and his lower jaw thrown considerably beneath the upper. Then he would cast himself into a chair, swing one of his legs over an arm of it, and commence his lecture in the most *outré* manner. The abruptness, however, never failed to command silence and rivet attention.

"'The Count was wounded in the arm—the bullet had sunk deep into the flesh—it was, however, extracted—and he is now in a fair way of recovery.' That will do very well for a novel, but it won't do for us, Gentlemen: for 'Sir Ralph Abercrombie received a ball in the thick part of his thigh, and it buried itself deep, deep: and it got among important parts, and it couldn't be felt; but the surgeons, nothing daunted, groped, and groped, and groped—and Sir Ralph died.'"

Then he would enter upon an admirable discourse on the nature of gunshot wounds, their peculiar character, the course they followed; and he would reprobate, in the strongest manner, the impropriety and danger of seeking after balls in deep-seated parts, or in the cavities of the human body. Then he would contrast the improvements that had been made by the moderns over the practice of the ancients; and by the relation of often ludicrous and always interesting anecdotes, fix the subject on the minds of his pupils in the most indelible manner. Dr. THOMAS JOSEPH PETTIGREW
Biographical Memoirs, 1840.

Those Were the Days

In the intervals of writing metaphysical treatises, restoring the finances of this country after the great Revolution, taking a part in the foundation of the Bank of England, instituting reforms in the administration of the Poor Law, and assisting in the framing of the Constitution of the State of Carolina, JOHN LOCKE found time to conduct a successful general practice.

Lancet, annotation.

The Young Claude Bernard

Claude Bernard lost his father at an early age, and to make a living had to take a job with a pharmacist who was also a veterinary surgeon. The first scepticism about matters medical came to him when he found that whenever a drug had fallen into disuse, "We must put it into the Theriac jar," they said. This was a complex pharmaceutical preparation obtained from mixing the bottom of the pots; good for many and varied uses, the therapeutic properties assigned to it remained constant, in spite of the variations in its composition.

Adapted from a lecture by Ch. Richet
Presse médicale, 1919.

Making Ends Meet

. . . the doctor who taught singing under the mustachioed and bearded guise of an Italian count, at a ladies' school at Chatham, in order that he might make his West End calls between 3 and 6 p.m. in a well-built brougham drawn by a fiery steed from a livery stables.

Old book.

[64]

George Crabbe

If Crabbe's schooling was scanty and his culture never wide, he early learnt things that books could never have taught him,

> *And all that boys acquire whom men neglect.*

Next followed apprenticeship to a series of surgeons; a rough experience, apt to include helping the surgeon's ploughboy at odd moments. Then, at seventeen, came romance. He fell in love with Sarah Elmy. The poem he addressed "To Mira" seems starchy and sickly enough to modern taste; it only shows how rash it is to accuse writers of "insincerity"; seldom has love proved truer. To win her he battled for twelve years against discouragement, poverty and debt. Twice he tried to make his way in London. His first attempt was in 1776-7, as a surgeon; but he was too poor to pay for proper teaching, and his efforts at self-help led to little result—except that his landlady, finding he had a dead baby in his cupboard, became convinced that he had dug up her William, buried the week before, and was only prevented from haling him to the Mansion House by the production of the child with its face, fortunately, still intact. It is clear that Crabbe was even less made for medicine than Keats; the idea of being called on to do a serious operation was a nightmare to him; and after struggling two years more with his profession at Aldborough he decided to abandon it and take the decisive step, as it proved, of his whole life.

F. L. Lucas
George Crabbe: an Anthology, 1933.

Richard Bright

He could not have been called a brilliant man. He made at first no great impression on those about him. But brilliancy is often ephemeral; very often brilliancy spells instability. Bright showed a steadfastness of purpose and an equanimity that are rarer and more precious than mere brilliancy. He was a simple, straightforward, kindly man, who met life with charity and tolerance and serenity; a conscientious, painstaking physician; a patient, careful, modest, scrupulous time-taking observer. He became a wise and learned man, and the fruits of his labours assure him a well-merited and honourable immortality.

Bright was buried in Bethnal Green. There is a tablet dedicated to his memory in St. James' Church in Piccadilly. The inscription ends with these words:

"He contributed to medical science many discoveries
and works of great value,
And died while in the full practice of his profession
after a life of warm affection
unsullied purity and great usefulness."

W. S. THAYER
B.M.J., 1927.

The Surgeon Desplein

Like all men of genius, he had no heirs; he carried everything in him, and carried it away with him. The glory of a surgeon is like that of an actor: they live only so long as they are alive, and their talent leaves no trace when they are gone. Actors and surgeons, like great singers too, like the executants who by their performance increase the power of music tenfold, are all the heroes of a moment.

BALZAC
La Messe de l'Athée.

Dr. John Clarke (died 1815)

Beneath this stone, shut up in the dark,
Lies a learned man-midwife, y'clep'd Doctor Clarke.
On earth while he lived, by attending men's wives,
He increased population some thousands of lives:
Thus a gain to the nation was gain to himself;
And enlarged population, enlargement of pelf.
So he toiled late and early, from morning till night,
The squalling of children his greatest delight.
Then worn out with *labours*, he died skin and bone,
And his ladies he left all to *Mansfield* and *Stone*.

> *Nugae Canorae*, or Epitaphian Mementos (in Stone-cutter's Verse) of the Medici Family of Modern Times.

" Derviche Guérisseur " (Dr. David Gruby, born in Hungary 1811)

A lady who suffered from intractable insomnia—one of those who "do not sleep a wink"—was ordered to take a spoonful of his famous water every half hour during the night. The nurse had no difficulty with the first two or three doses. But when the fourth was presented, the indignant lady insisted on being allowed to sleep in peace.

He was called to a paralysed patient. He found her immobilised in her airchair. "What oil do you use in your kitchen?" "Why, ordinary oil, I suppose." "Can I see it?" When the bottle was produced, Gruby uncorked it and calmly began emptying it on the carpet. The patient jumped up: "Here, that's a Persian rug." The rug was ruined—the lady cured.

Dr. GUSTAV MONOD
Lancet, 1926.

Thomas Addison

In the year 1855 Thomas Addison, one of the greatest clinical observers which this country has produced, published a description of *The Constitutional and Local Effects of Disease of the Suprarenal Capsules*. In the preface to his pamphlet— one of the classics of medical literature—after pointing out that the pathologist may sometimes be able to throw much light upon the functions of diseased organs, and that we are apt to forget how much of our physiological knowledge has been revealed by casual observations of the effects of disease, he goes on to speak of the adrenals, and adds: "It is as a first and feeble step towards inquiry into the functions and influence of these organs, suggested by pathology, that I now put forth the following pages." Yet that "feeble step" was destined to be epoch-making; for Addison's description of the disease which goes by his name was the starting-point of our present knowledge of the functions of the endocrine glands.

Let us pause, then, to consider how Addison set to work. He noticed that a certain group of symptoms was apt to occur in association—namely, anaemia, debility, remarkable feebleness of the heart's action, irritability of the stomach, and a peculiar dingy or smoky discoloration of the skin— and that in every case in which this syndrome was met with extensive disease of the adrenals was found *post mortem*. So constant was this association that, in the later cases of the series, the disease of the adrenals was predicted during the lifetime of the sufferer.

Sir ARCHIBALD GARROD
B.M.J., 1926.

The Good Old Days before Lister

When it rages in a great hospital it is like a plague; few who are seized with it can escape. There is no hospital, however small, airy, or well regulated, where this epidemic ulcer is not to be found at times; then no operation dare be performed. Every cure stands still. Every wound becomes a sore, and every sore is apt to run into gangrene. It has been named the Hospital Gangrene; and such were its ravages in the Hôtel-Dieu of Paris (that great storehouse of corruption and disease) that the surgeons did not dare to call it by its true name; they called it the rottenness, foulness, sloughing of the sore. The word hospital gangrene they durst not pronounce, for it sounded like a death-knell; at the hearing of that ominous word the patients gave themselves up for lost. In the Hôtel-Dieu this gangrene raged without inter-mission for two hundred years, till of late, under the new Government of France, the hospital has been reformed. A young surgeon (says an ancient French author) who is bred in the Hôtel-Dieu, may learn the various forms of incisions, operations too, and the manner of dressing wounds, but the way of curing wounds he cannot learn. Every patient he takes in hand (do what he will) must die of gangrene.

JOHN BELL (of Edinburgh)
Principles of Surgery, 1801.

Lister on Himself

I must not expect to be a Liston or a Syme, still I shall get on. Certain it is, I love Surgery more and more, and this is one great point; and I believe my judgment is pretty sound, which is another important point. Also I trust I am honest, and a lover of truth, which is perhaps as important as any-thing. As to brilliant talent, I know I do not possess it; but I must try to make up as far as I can by perseverance.

LISTER, *in a letter to his father*, 1854.

[69]

What Some of Them Thought of Lister

After graduating in Edinburgh in 1874, Rutherford Morison was house surgeon at the Royal Infirmary to Patrick Heron Watson, a surgeon who was bitterly opposed to Joseph Lister and "his newfangled method." Morison spent as much time as was possible, and as much as he dare without being detected by his chief, in Lister's ward; he used to relate that the feeling on the part of his chief was so great that had his "disloyalty" been discovered he knew it would have meant instant dismissal.

Obituary notice of Rutherford Morison
B.M.J., 1939.

A Casual Walk

One of the great romances of surgery is concerned with the almost casual manner in which during a walk Dr. Thomas Anderson, Professor of Chemistry at Glasgow, mentioned to Lister the researches of Pasteur which dealt with questions of fermentation and putrefaction. The papers written by Pasteur were not only new in statement, but new-fangled. They were unconventional; and convention, the daughter of attainment but the mother of scepticism and decadence, is often inspired by a zeal for denial. Her motto should be "Ich bin der Geist der stets verneint." As seems inevitable, therefore, these articles had been generally received with scepticism, ridicule, or indifference. To Lister, however, they made an instant appeal, for he seemed to realise in a moment their strict relevance to the problem of infection in wounds. His search for an ideal or perfect method of treating wounds—a method which would exclude or destroy the "all-pervading vibrios" which he was convinced were the cause of "putrefaction"—began forthwith.

LORD MOYNIHAN
B.M.J., 1930.

He was nearly six feet in height, upright, well knit, com-
pactly built, deep chested. His touch in manipulation was
delicate, and he taught the importance of avoiding any
roughness or bruising of the tissues. He was a slow, careful
and deliberate operator. His bearing was dignified, and his
manner invariably courteous, but with the natural restraint
of a serious and sincere soul, for it had a certain aloofness in
it. But he was very responsive, and his manner had no
tinge of being forced, artificial or affected. I cannot imagine
his being on easy terms with anyone who was not a colleague,
a co-worker or a pupil, or someone with whom he might
be sharing common interests in science, art, nature or travel.
He agreed with Goethe that "die Arbeit macht die Gesellen,"
it is working together which makes fellowship. He enjoyed
travelling and took long vacations abroad; but complete
idleness never appealed to him. On his holidays he had
addresses to prepare or proofs to correct; and he carried with
him, and could always fall back on, a volume of Horace,
Dante or Goethe. He fished a little, but was never an expert.
His efforts at skating were limited to figures of 8's or 3's,
but of small dimensions! He took great pleasure in walks
and in studying bird life. Golf and Bridge, in those days,
had not eaten too deeply into the other interests of life. A
great trait in his character was his invariable gentleness and
sympathy with the humblest or roughest of his hospital
patients. He seldom referred to a patient as "a case," but
introduced his remarks with such kindly terms as "this poor
fellow," or "this good woman," or "this little child."

ST. CLAIR THOMPSON
Edinburgh Med. J., 1942.

Lister and the Children

Once a small urchin in the wards, as his eyes followed Lister's movements, confided to a bystander, "It's us wee yins he likes best, and next it's the auld women."

H. C. CAMERON
B.M.J., 1948.

Lister as a Patient saw Him

His brow spreads large and placid, and his eye
Is deep and bright, with steady looks that still.
Soft lines of tranquil thought his face fulfil—
His face at once benign and proud and shy.
If envy scout, if ignorance deny
His faultless patience, his unyielding will,
Beautiful gentleness and splendid skill,
Innumerable gratitudes reply.
His wise, rare smile is sweet with certainties,
And seems in all his patients to compel
Such love and faith as failure cannot quell.

W. E. HENLEY (once his patient in the
Edinburgh Royal Infirmary, 1873).

Sir James Paget

Paget's love for brevity was well known to his friends. He never used two words when one was sufficient. Once he was challenged to a sort of contest in brevity, and accepted the challenge. His adversary was a Yorkshireman, who came into his consulting room, and merely thrust out his lips, saying "What's that?" "That's cancer," he answered. "And what's to be done with it?" "Cut it out." "What's your fee?" "Two guineas." "You must make a deal o' money at that rate." And there the consultation ended.

R. H. MAJOR
Classic Descriptions of Disease.

Dr. Fuller of George's

Fuller was a practical, able, careful and painstaking physician who took from his kinsfolk of the great firm of general practitioners, Fuller and Hammerton of Piccadilly, a strong bent towards pharmaceutical methods. I was Fuller's clerk for three or four months, and learned much of an empirical sort from him; and, moreover, the methods of minute diagnosis of disease of the chest, then comparatively new. After a thorough examination of the patient, Fuller would draw himself up, extract a handsome gold pen from his pocket, dip it cautiously into the inkpot and recite, as he wrote down in a fine hand, an imposing prescription for a mixture of many drugs; and then another for a no less universal pill. Then came the diet and the alcohol. Every patient at St. George's had his liquor as a routine, his four or six ounces of port or sherry (often a good deal more), when in peril of death a liberal ration of brandy, and when convalescent his ale. The cellars of the hospital at that day were filled with wines and brandy by the hogshead, and with ales by the tun. We never heard of anything so vulgar as whisky. Fuller was not a genius by any means, but he was a kindly, competent, and diligent man, and a fair teacher of whom I retain a grateful memory.

Sir CLIFFORD ALLBUTT
Lancet, 1922.

Ronald Ross

To combat malaria, Sir Ronald Ross did not indeed erect an altar; no, he oiled a pond—making libation to its presiding genii.

Sir OLIVER LODGE
British Association, 1913.

Dr. Bence Jones

. . . the brilliant Bence Jones, one so brilliant that I have
waited a while to give him his due place. Of his pioneer
work in biochemistry it is not my purpose, and hardly
within my competency to speak. Clinical teacher he was not,
he did not pretend to be. For this reason, and because of
his scandalous unpunctuality, there was no competition for
his clerkship; so I was left to hold the post, save for my Fuller
interlude, during all the rest of my time at St. George's.
Bence Jones told me again and again that I was a fool for
this continuous attachment to him, and so perhaps I was;
but the man was fascinating, and from his brilliant personality one gained much inspiration. As I used to stand waiting
at the stairhead, I see him vividly now, bounding up the
steps two or three at a time, an hour or an hour and a half
too late, the morning's guineas (so men said) scattering out
of his pockets as he flew; first appeared the silvery head,
then the handsome presence, the sanguine and vivid countenance, the blue eyes; then came the bound towards the
beds, and the sharp question—"Which are the worst cases,
let me see?" Next, hasty as it all was, the rapid snatch at my
poor notes, the kindly penetrating glance at the patient, the
almost magical rapidity of a diagnosis rapped out in half a
dozen words, and generally right; then the bedcard, and
the scratchy prescription of his invariable pot. nit. and mint
water, and the dash on to the next bed. Here perchance
arose a conflict of evidence; the bedcard and pen were hurled
upon the bed, and we heard the frequent chiding phrase—
"O! Medical facts! Medical facts!" yet all with a dancing
blue eye and a merry, petulant face.

In therapeutics, or rather in pharmaceutics, Bence Jones
was an utter sceptic; or ought I rather to say a cool watcher
of unviolated nature? As a biochemist, he believed in nothing
he could not separate, test, and measure. Empirical experi-

[74]

ence, tradition, authority, routine, he disregarded or scorned. *Medical* facts! *Medical* facts! was his continual jibe. Extravagant, even whimsical, as all this was, it was nevertheless a sharp and an inspiring discipline at that time. Moreover, there were the happy days when Bence Jones, who was well known among foreign professors, would bring one of them to the wards, when a lively, interesting and more patient discussion would ensue, to the enjoyment and invaluable experience of his one St. George's disciple. It is hard to conceive a more striking contrast than this between my two teachers; the gentle fertilising rain of Fuller and the sheet lightning of Bence Jones. At last, on one sad day of a new session, sad to me, for I loved the man, he came up the familiar staircase, not swiftly, but slowly; and a wistful look upon his handsome face spoke of some tribulation. On reaching England from a Continental tour he had felt short of breath; in a shop in Dover he bought a binaural stethoscope, then a new toy, listened to his own heart, and heard a mitral systolic murmur. It may, perhaps, have been significant of subacute malignant endocarditis; for he did not live long afterwards. He was a noble gentleman; joy be to his soul; peace that eager spirit would not have desired.

Sir CLIFFORD ALLBUTT
Lancet, 1922.

Prophet Without Honour—Sir James Mackenzie

When I took the manuscript to him at his house in Bentinck St. he gave me a copy of his epoch-making book on *The Pulse*, which had been published in 1902. He said, "I have to give it away. Nobody will buy it."

Sir ARTHUR HURST
A Twentieth-Century Physician.

[75]

Picture of a G.P.

He may not be able to excise a Gasserian ganglion, or know very much about the researches of Calmette or von Pircquet. But he knows precisely when to call in the men who do. And he's just the sort of assistant with whom they feel safe in setting out to work. While, on the other hand, upon a hundred points—little, everyday problems of medical practice, unclassified ailments that have never got into the text-books or been dignified with a Latin name, doubtful beginnings of more definite illnesses, their home-treatment, and the adequate settlement of the domestic problems that they involve—there isn't a man in Harley Street who could give a more valuable opinion.

Such men are not only the pillars of our profession, but its topmost pinnacles, even if the wreaths and the knighthoods but seldom come their way. . . .

PETER HARDING, M.D.
The Corner of Harley Street.

The G.P.

He presides at birth and is sought in death, he knows of the skeleton which is hidden in most cupboards, he knows the tragedies which blast a life, and the minor discords which embitter it, he sees human virtue and human frailty, joy and sorrow, life in its seaminess and life in its excellence. Well for him if he can preserve a genial toleration for the frailties of mankind, and the spirit of charity. The contrary might be expected: as it is put by the Shepherd in *Noctes Ambrosianae*:

"Physicians, one might think, seein' folk deeing nicht and day in a' manner o' agonies, and bein' accustomed to pocket fees by the death-bed-side, would become in the core o' their hearts as callous as custocks."

Dr. J. PEARSE
Lancet, 1919.

Dr. John Byrom

... The attractive John Byrom (1691-1763) managed to combine in his life medicine, shorthand, mysticism, Toryism, Jacobitism, and wit, together with unceasing pen. He wrote quantities of prose and verse and published none of it. His engaging journals and his likeable poems have been made fully available by the Chatham Society. Of his longer effusions we must say here nothing except to note that he was both a witty poet and a fluent paraphraser. I cannot forgive him his attempt to versify the Advent Collect, as I believe that to be the noblest short complete piece of prose in English. His attempt fails as it deserves. A more memorable failure is the attempt to versify the prayer for all sorts and conditions of men; for it begins with this couplet:

It will bear repeating again and again
Will that prayer for all sorts and conditions of men;

lines that so instantly recall the once famous advertisement

They come as a boon and a blessing to men,
The Pickwick, the Owl, and the Waverley pen,

that we can hardly read further, and, indeed, must not. His hymns proper are few and unsuccessful. But there are two, called *The Desponding Soul's Wish* and *The Answer*, which deserve attention for the metrical device, recalling some of the old French poems, which makes the last line of each stanza the first of the next. He tries hymns for all the church seasons, and fails except in one, for his second attempt at a poem on the Nativity gives us the one hymn that preserves his name:

Christians, awake, salute the happy morn
Whereon the Saviour of the world was born.

GEORGE SAMPSON
Seven Essays.

[77]

Portrait of the Doctor

The world has long ago decided that you have no working hours which anybody is bound to respect, and nothing except your extreme bodily illness will excuse you in its eyes from refusing to help a man, who thinks he may need your help, at any hour of the day or night. Nobody will care whether you are in your bed, or in your bath, or at the theatre. If any one of the children of men has a pain or a hurt in him you will be summoned; and, as you know, what little vitality you may have accumulated in your leisure will be dragged out of you again.

In all time of flood, fire, famine, plague, pestilence, battle, murder, and sudden death it will be required of you that you report for duty at once, and go on duty at once, and that you stay on duty until your strength fails you or your conscience relieves you; whichever may be the longer period. . . . Have you heard of any Bill for an eight hours' day for doctors?

You belong to the privileged classes. May I remind you of some of your privileges? You and Kings are the only people whose explanation the Police will accept if you exceed the legal limit in your car. On presentation of your visiting-card you can pass through the most turbulent crowd unmolested and even with applause. If you fly a yellow flag over a centre of population you can turn it into a desert. If you choose to fly a Red Cross flag over a desert you can turn it into a centre of population towards which, as I have seen, men will crawl on hands and knees. You can forbid any ship to enter any port in the world. If you think it necessary to the success of any operation in which you are interested, you can stop a 20,000-ton liner with mails in mid-ocean till the operation is concluded. You can order whole quarters of a city to be pulled down or burnt up; and you can trust to the armed co-operation of the nearest troops to see that your prescriptions are properly carried out.

KIPLING

"A Doctor's Work," from *A Book of Words.*

Sir Henry Acland (*Regius Professor at Oxford*)

His writing was even more illegible than that of most busy doctors in the days when medical secretaries were almost unknown. The wife of one of the Canons of Christ Church had invited Acland to dinner, but was quite unable to decipher his reply. The Canon suggested that she should take the letter to a chemist in the High, who would certainly be able to read the Regius Professor's writing in view of the many prescriptions of his he was daily called upon to dispense. The chemist was accordingly asked to interpret the letter. He retired with it to the back of the shop. Five minutes later he reappeared. "That will be half-a-crown," he said, as he handed the lady a bottle of medicine.

Sir ARTHUR HURST
A Twentieth-Century Physician.

Wilfred Trotter

In the outpatient department which it was his pleasure to attend to the end of his time, it was his habit to listen attentively to the longest and most rambling story, alike from the neurotic and the husky old slum lady, with the same courtesy that he probably paid to duchesses, a group of patients whom, unlike some eminent doctors, he was never heard to mention. He never interrupted but gradually led by agreement and sympathetic inquiry to things that might be important for the matter in hand. This charming delicacy of approach to the mind and personality was then equalled by the extreme gentleness of his physical examination, for I think I never saw him hurt a patient. . . . His subsequent dissection of the story and often of the patient's mind was apt to be amusingly destructive, sometimes by no means strait-laced, and if the patient had been a thought superior, perhaps as contemptuous as his handling had been courteous.

Obituary notice.

Strange Obsession

Mr. Sheridan at the time lived in Bedford Street opposite Henrietta Street, which ranges with the south side of Covent Garden, so that the prospect lies open the whole way free of interruption: we were standing together at the drawing-room window expecting Johnson who was to dine there. Mr. Sheridan asked me could I see the length of the garden. "No, sir!" "Take out your opera-glass, Johnson is coming; you may know him by his gait." I perceived him at a good distance working along with a peculiar solemnity of deportment, and an awkward sort of measured step; at that time the broad flagging on each side of the streets was not universally adopted, and stone posts were in fashion to prevent the annoyance of carriages. Upon every post as he passed along, I could observe he deliberately laid his hand; but missing one of them, when he had got at some distance, he seemed suddenly to recollect himself, and immediately returning back, carefully performed the accustomed ceremony, and resumed his former course, not omitting one till he gained the crossing. This, Mr. Sheridan assured me, however odd it might appear, was his constant practice: but why or wherefore he could not inform me.

WHITE
Miscellany, 1799.

Déjerine

He summarised his methods in these words: "Expliquer au malade, après lui avoir fait confesser sa vie, comment et pourquoi il est tombé malade, comment et pourquoi il arrivera à se guérir."

Sir ARTHUR HURST
A Twentieth-Century Physician.

The New Broom

Patients who had chronic diseases or whose lives had long been worn threadbare, like old Featherstone's, had been at once inclined to try him; also, many who did not like paying their doctor's bills, thought agreeably of opening an account with a new doctor and sending for him without stint if the children's temper wanted a dose, occasions when the old practitioners were often crusty; and all persons thus inclined to employ Lydgate held it likely that he was clever. Some considered that he might do more than others "where there was liver";—at least there would be no harm in getting a few bottles of "stuff" from him, since if these proved useless it would still be possible to return to the Purifying Pills, which kept you alive, if they did not remove the yellowness.

GEORGE ELIOT
Middlemarch.

An Obstinate Old Lady

I recall one stout old lady who made a most unexpected recovery, nor could I find the reason until long afterwards when she told me that one of her daughters had come bringing a shroud and saying to her, "You'll be wanting this very soon, Mother." This so infuriated the old body that she made up her mind to get better in order to cut the daughter out of her will—which she did!

Dr. W. N. LEAK
Practitioner, 1948.

Laënnec's Background

René Théophile Hyacinthe Laënnec was born on the
17th February 1781, the year which saw Johnson's *Lives of
the Poets*, and the second and third volumes of Gibbon's
Decline and Fall. Wordsworth was a lad of eleven. Napoleon,
a little older, was already two years on with his military
education at Brienne. John Hunter was in his prime at
fifty-three. Seven years before, Priestley announced the
discovery of oxygen. Albrecht von Haller, the "prince of
physiologists," died four years ago. Morgagni had already
been dead ten years. But the most important date near by
was that, nineteen years earlier, on which Rousseau's *Contrat
Social* appeared; and his opening words, "Man is born free
and is everywhere in chains" had not been lost upon his
generation. Adam Smith had taught something of the
wealth of nations; Voltaire had outraged established orders
and amused the others; and Burke was still in his grandest
vein. No one had any reason to suppose that the infant son
of a Breton country lawyer was destined to reach an equally
enduring fame. Certainly the good people of Quimper, the
little port about thirty miles from Brest, could not have
guessed. For the Laënnecs, though respectable Celts and
reputable lawyers, had never achieved anything but a local
name; and in point of fact, René's father was a rather
shiftless improvident character who neglected his family and
lived on his sons later in life.

Dr. CLIFFORD HOYLE
Brit. J. Tuberc., 1944.

Laënnec

Laënnec was thirty-seven when he wrote his book *De
l'Auscultation Médiate*, a thin meditative man of about five
feet three, with chiselled features, high cheek bones, a long

head, light brown hair and blue-grey eyes. He was neither handsome nor robust. Also one imagines he was rather shy and aloof, a little austere, lacking a keen sense of humour, and thus not one of those to whom success comes easily. Negelect at home as a child and dependence on his uncle, acting on a temperament naturally reserved, must have made him chary of the world at large. But his power of application and sincerity were immense, and seem to have left few who came in contact with him in any doubt about his greatness. There was nothing flamboyant, nothing ostentatious, about Laënnec. Throughout life he remained simple in his tastes, content with very little in the way of personal comforts and amusements, and wrapped in his work. In what time he spared, he learnt to play the flute very well, danced a bit, read widely in the classics, and rambled in the countryside near Paris or by the shores of his native Brittany. He was hardly versatile as some great men have been. His memorable work dealt with one branch of medicine only. Nor was he particularly learned in an academic sense. He was, essentially, a pioneer; and like many pioneers, he had penetration rather than range, depth rather than breadth, an immense grasp of detail rather than that kind of ability which roves more superficially through large tracts of knowledge. We know that he was well aware of his own ignorance on many things, and readily confessed it. But on the subject of his own choice he made the knowledge of others seem like the simplicity of the child or the savage. For in a few brief crowded years he fashioned the science of diagnosis of diseases of the chest so completely that, as Lawrason Brown truly said, "he who now adds a single stone to the structure is deservedly acclaimed by his fellows."

Dr. CLIFFORD HOYLE
Brit. J. Tuberc., 1944.

[83]

An Amiable Surgeon

> Stay Passenger and view this stone,
> For under it lyis such a one
> Who cuired many whil he lieved;
> So gratious he noe man grieved:
> Yea when his physicke force oft failed
> His plesant purpose then prevailed;
> For of his God he got the grace
> To live in mirth, and die in peace:
> Heavin hes his soule, his corps this stone
> Sigh, passenger, and soe be gone.

> *Epitaph of Dr. Peter Lowe, 1550-1610 in the*
> *Cathedral churchyard of Glasgow, quoted by*
> *Pennant, 1612—said to have been written by*
> *George Baker, surgeon ordinary to Queen*
> *Elizabeth.*

Sir Astley Cooper

Imagine a tall, elegantly formed man, moderately robust, with a remarkably pleasing and striking countenance, red and fresh as a rose, apparently about fifty-eight or sixty years of age, but in reality above seventy, very agile and graceful in all his movements, simply but handsomely attired, with the spirit and vivacity and bearing of a youth, with in short no marks of advanced age except a head as white as the driven snow—and a very just conception may be formed of the appearance of Sir Astley Cooper.

WILLIAM GIBSON, M.D.
Rambles in Europe in 1839.

[84]

Two Rules of Practice

An old Scotch physician for whom I had a great respect and whom I frequently met professionally in the city used to say, as we were entering the patient's room together, "Weel, Mister Cooper, we ha' only twa things to keep in meend, and they'll searve us for here and herea'ter; one is always to have the fear of the Laird before our een; that 'ill do for herea'ter; and the t'other is to keep your booels open, and that will do for here."

Sir ASTLEY COOPER
Lectures on Surgery, 1824.

" Physician "

Few ways of life were hidden from Physician, and he was oftener in its darkest places than even Bishop. There were brilliant ladies about London who perfectly doted on him, my dear, as the most charming creature and the most delightful person, who would have been shocked to find themselves so close to him if they could have known on what sights those thoughtful eyes of his had rested within an hour or two, and near to whose beds, and under what roofs, his composed figure had stood. But, Physician was a composed man, who performed neither on his own trumpet, nor on the trumpets of other people. Many wonderful things did he see and hear, and much irreconcilable moral contradiction did he pass his life among; yet his equality of compassion was no more disturbed than the Divine Master's of all healing was. He went like the rain, among the just and the unjust, doing all the good he could, and neither proclaiming it in the synagogues nor at the corners of streets.

DICKENS
Little Dorrit.

Horehound Tea Keeps a Saint Out of Heaven

In the autumn of 1800 I was asked if I wished to see a triumphant saint expire. "Much more," I replied, "than to see Rome in all her pristine or present glory." I was accordingly directed to call on Mrs. W—— of the Surrey-road, which I did, in whom I beheld the nearest approach to an animated skeleton I ever expected to see. She instantly recognised me (having often met me at the sanctuary), and shook hands feebly.

Mr. Sutleffe had the cruelty to administer horehound tea, which prevented the saint from "going home." When informed that she was out of danger, she shed tears of grief. She has retired to Warwickshire instead of Paradise, and is got quite lusty.

> EDWARD SUTLEFFE
> *Medical and Surgical Cases, selected during a practice of thirty-eight years,* 1824.
> (With a comment by the Medico-Chirurgical Review.)

Lisfranc of Paris

He is a big, burly, narrow-shouldered man, more than six feet high, negligent in dress, awkward in gait, uncouth in manners, and loud and boisterous in discourse. In his lectures he is said to be so unsparing of his brethren, and in hospital practice so harsh towards his patients, as to be unpopular with both. I cannot say whether those charges are well founded, but am inclined to believe them exaggerated, inasmuch as I saw nothing beyond the natural want of polish in the man (increased, I thought, by affectation of wishing to appear worse than he really was) from which I should have drawn such a conclusion. I was seated with a bevy of young medical friends beneath the boughs of a wide spreading elm, on a delightful summer morning, the 18th of June, and saw him for the first time, as he entered the hospital gate, and sauntered slowly along the gravelled walk of the long and wide avenue leading to the ward containing his female patients. His head, covered with a rusty black and red cap, which in the shape of a tea-cup stuck like a plaster to the summit of his crown; his long-waisted scanty snuff-coloured coat dangling about his heels and tapering away to sharpness, like the tail of a kite; his curiously contrived pantaloons loose and bagging about his hips, and at each stride fluttering to the wind; his long shovel-shaped shoes scattering pebbles as he walked from right to left; his arms standing out from his body like the handle of a pump, conjoined with his outstretched flexible neck, which swung to and fro beneath the pressure of his lengthy and wedge-shaped visage, presented one of the most ludicrous spectacles I ever beheld. He cast an enquiring sideways glance at our group as he passed, which seemed to indicate, I thought, a belief that we were amusing ourselves at his expense, for he instantly bristled up, and with averted head hurried out of sight. . . . He called the roll to ascertain that all his *internes* or house pupils were mustered at their posts, and refused to proceed until a delinquent who was in bed taking a morning nap was brought to the scene of action. He then began a clinical discourse, explaining the general nature of the diseases before him, waxing warmer and warmer as he proceeded, and gradually raising his stentorian voice until its tones seemed to shake the foundations of the old building and startle the very rafters above our heads; whilst he, peering and scanning from right to left the looks of his auditors with great self-satisfaction, seemed to enquire into the effect his sesqui-pedalian words and thundering sentences may have produced upon their minds.

WILLIAM GIBSON, M.D.
Rambles in Europe in 1839.

[87]

Of William Butler Practitioner of Physic (born 1535)

A Clergyman in Cambridgeshire, by excessive application in composing a learned sermon which he was to preach before the King at Newmarket, had brought himself into such a way that he could not sleep. His friends were advised to give him opium, which he took in so large a quantity that it threw him into a profound lethargy. Dr. Butler was sent for from Cambridge: who, upon seeing and hearing his case, flew into a passion, and told his wife that she was in danger of being hanged for killing her husband, and very abruptly left the room. As he was going through the yard, in his return home, he saw several cows, and asked her to whom they belonged: she said, to her husband. Will you, says the Doctor, give me one of these cows if I restore him to life? She replied, with all my heart. He presently ordered a cow to be killed, and the patient to be put into the warm carcase, which in a short time recovered him.

GRANGER
Biographical History, 1769.

Velpeau

There can be no doubt that the surgeon of La Charité is not deficient in originality and power of invention, and that moreover he possesses a very extended knowledge of every subject that he treats of. But whenever these two qualities are brought prominently forward by an author, we very generally find that one proves injurious to the other. Now this is what occurs to M. Velpeau. He aims to pass for very learned; and his lectures, like his writings, and we may add his practice too, present a living panorama of whatever is new abroad as well as in France. He has been aptly called *the great experimenter of the present time,* applying whatever others propose and applying it, too, with a certain spirit of modification, if not of improvement. This arises from a disposition in his character to appropriate to himself every suggestion that he at all modifies, and to give a decided preference of his own manner of seeing and doing things to that of the original proposers. Now from this habit, praise-worthy we admit in principle, arise certain inconveniences which it may be worth while to note. M. Velpeau often does not make himself sufficient master of every subject that he canvasses and comments upon. Belonging to the school of sentiment rather than to that of experience, he judges of things at once and from his first impressions, instead of waiting for the results of a complete and rigorous examination. In matters of actual practice he is guided in the same manner. More ruled by the wish to improve than thoroughly to understand, he does not study with sufficient attention the various processes and methods which he applies; he persuades himself that what others have done is neither novel nor important, and whatever change he introduces acquires in his eyes a *brevet* of invention and a right of personal property. This mode of seeing and doing things gives to the honourable professor a seeming want of gravity and of good faith, and accounts for the numerous accusations which have been brought against him. Perhaps these reflections are applicable rather to the encyclopediacal character of his mind and of his mode of instruction, than to his teaching itself. Certain it is that if his lectures aimed less at being so comprehensive, they would gain in accuracy and profundity what they lost in the novelty and variety of their details.

M. Guerin
Gazette Médicale, 1840.

Beethoven

Apart from minor ailments, such as whitlow, which interfered with playing the piano, and a moderate degree of myopia, Beethoven began to suffer at a comparatively early date from symptoms of cirrhosis of the liver, for which indulgence in punch was probably responsible. In his later years oedema of the legs and ascites developed, giving rise to dyspnoeal attacks from pressure on the abdomen. Paracentesis abdominis was performed on four occasions, but relief was only temporary, and death took place at the age of 56. The necropsy, which was performed by Dr. Johannes Wagner, of the Vienna Pathological Museum, showed atrophy of the auditory nerves and atrophic cirrhosis of the liver.

Lancet, *annotation*.

Liston

Though, seemingly, of robust frame and great strength of constitution, he is so solicitous of preserving his health and is so confident of the value of active exercise on horseback as for a long time to have kept hunters and a pack of hounds, which while he lived at Edinburgh he exercised at daybreak and long before most of his brethren were out of bed. It is said he has now abandoned the sport, having fractured his pelvis and nearly broken his neck at some inordinate leap, and since that period has followed the exercise of a boatman on the Thames, by rowing every morning several miles before breakfast. He has a passion for domestic animals—horses, dogs and cats. His enormous black cat, *Tom*, is almost as well known in London as Liston himself, being not infrequently mounted alongside his master in the splendid chariot, and a constant guest at his hospitable board, where I had the honour of forming his acquaintance by finding his foot in my soup before aware of its proximity to my plate.

WILLIAM GIBSON, M.D.
Rambles in Europe in 1839.

A Bad Business

In 1839 Lady Flora Hastings was on duty at Court performing the functions of a lady-in-waiting upon Queen Victoria when her appearance suggested to some of her associates that she might be with child. One of them reported her suspicions to Sir James Clark, the Court physician, who at once fell in with the insinuation, and after catechising her, intimated that she "must be privately married, or at best ought to be so." This Lady Flora indignantly denied, and to indicate her character, demanded a consultation. Lord Melbourne reluctantly permitted a medical examination to be made, which at once established her chastity. Sir James Clark and Sir Charles Clarke the consultant, certified that "there are no grounds for believing that pregnancy does exist, or ever has existed." Lady Flora survived this humiliating ordeal only a few months.

Dr. ROBERT FORBES
B.M.J., 1935.

Dupuytren

As to Dupuytren, he seldom speaks except to abuse a dresser or a nurse. On the history, present state, or probable termination of the patient's case, he seldom utters a word; and it is with regret that we are obliged to add that the conduct of a man whose name ranks so high in the profession should be, towards his pupils, more like the demeanour of a general to his soldiers, than that of a teacher to whom they look up with reverence and respect. What can be gained by running round the wards of a hospital with a snarling surgeon who so far occasionally loses sight of the conduct which one gentleman should observe to another, as to express his disapprobation by a kick on the shins, or a "*donnez-vous place!*"? Attendance on hospital practice, as it is called in this country, is one of the principal means which a young man has of studying his profession, and what can he be expected to know if the persons on whom he relies for information should seal up their mouths in sullen obstinacy, or deliver their opinions in such dogmatic confidence as to deter a pupil from asking a second question?

Dr. FREDERICK AUGUSTUS AMMON
A Parallel of French and German Surgery, 1823.

Queen Victoria's Abscess

(After Cameron became a student at Guy's in 1902 he liked to remember that Lister twice asked him to dinner. On the first occasion his father was staying with Lister at Park Crescent; on the second he was alone, and Lister told him in somewhat greater detail than was given in Godlee's book the story of the first use of rubber drainage tubes in surgery.) He said that he was hurriedly summoned to Balmoral to treat Queen Victoria, who had developed an abscess. On arrival he made the necessary incision and inserted a wick to help the drainage. The result was not satisfactory; her temperature rose and she suffered great pain and discomfort. As he walked in the grounds of Balmoral—whenever Lister had a problem to settle he walked, pondering the situation— he thought of a possible device. He had brought with him a primitive form of his carbolic spray—Richardson's "atomizer"—to which was attached a long piece of rubber tube. Returning to the castle, he cut off a suitable length of this rubber tube and soaked it all night in a 1 in 20 solution of carbolic acid, using a soap dish in his bedroom for the purpose. In the morning he inserted it and found that it answered its purpose so well that recovery quickly followed. "If," added Lister, "you ever hear anyone complaining that in hospitals patients are sometimes experimented upon, you may think of that story though you must not tell it."

Dr. H. C. CAMERON
B.M.J., 1948.

[92]

Sir Ralph Bloomfield Bonington

Sir Ralph Bloomfield Bonington wafts himself into the room. He is a tall man, with a head like a tall and slender egg. He has been in his time a slender man; but now, in his sixth decade, his waistcoat has filled out somewhat. His fair eyebrows arch good-naturedly and uncritically. He has a most musical voice; his speech is a perpetual anthem; and he never tires of the sound of it. He radiates an enormous self-satisfaction, cheering, reassuring, healing by the mere incompatibility of disease or anxiety with his welcome presence. Even broken bones, it is said, have been known to unite at the sound of his voice: he is a born healer, as independent of mere treatment and skill as any Christian scientist. When he expands into oratory or scientific exposition, he is as energetic as Walpole; but it is with a bland, voluminous, atmospheric energy, which envelops its subject and its audience, and makes interruption or inattention impossible, and imposes veneration and credulity on all but the strongest minds. He is known in the medical world as B.B.; and the envy roused by his success in practice is softened by the conviction that he is, scientifically considered, a colossal humbug: the fact being that, though he knows just as much (and just as little) as his contemporaries, the qualifications that pass muster in common men reveal their weakness when hung on his egregious personality.

GEORGE BERNARD SHAW
The Doctor's Dilemma.

Osler's Personal Ideals

I have had three personal ideals. One, to do the day's work well and not to bother about tomorrow. The second ideal has been to act the Golden Rule, as far as in me lay, toward my professional brethren and towards the patients committed to my care. And the third has been to cultivate such a measure of equanimity as would enable me to bear success with humility, the affection of my friends without pride, and to be ready when the day of sorrow and grief come to meet it with courage befitting a man.

> OSLER, *in his Speech in May,* 1905, *at the Farewell Dinner of the Medical profession of America and Canada, when he was bound for Oxford.*

Ripeness is All

When in 1932 Sir Thomas Barlow (aged 86) gave the address at the memorial service in the Guy's Hospital Chapel to Sir Charters Symonds, who had died at the ripe age of eighty, he was heard to murmur after reading the inscription on the coffin, " Poor fellow ! Poor fellow ! Cut off in the prime of life. Poor fellow ! "

> Sir ARTHUR HURST
> *A Twentieth-Century Physician.*

Byron's Last Illness

According to the accepted story, Byron died of a rheumatic fever at Missolonghi, induced by rowing in an open boat across the lagoon after being heated by riding and drenched by a thunderstorm. His doctors are accused of having failed to diagnose his illness and of having bled him to death. The facts do not confirm this theory. People forget to mention that on Feb. 15, 1824, two months before his death, Byron was struck down by a convulsive fit, which he himself, perhaps incorrectly, assumed to be epileptic. On the advice of Major Parry, he treated himself for this affliction by drinking enormous quantities of cider laced with strong insertions of brandy: I cannot believe that in the paludal climate of Missolonghi that was a wise thing to do. It is quite true that in April he was drenched in a thunderstorm and that two days later he went out riding on a saddle which was still wet. Yet if his ten days' illness, which lasted from April 9 to April 19, was in fact rheumatic fever it is strange that he did not suffer the intense pain associated with that illness and even more strange that he was able on April 14 to walk unassisted from one room to the other. Nor is there any mention in the many accounts of his illness either of the heavy perspiration or of the swelling joints which rheumatic fever, as I understand, invariably produces. I am advised indeed by those experts whom I have consulted, that Byron's final illness must have been either typhoid or pernicious malaria.

And what about the famous accusation that Drs. Bruno and Van Millingen bled their patient to death? They may have wished to bleed him copiously, but they did not succeed. Obstinately he refused to be bled until almost the last moment, remarking, perhaps not inappropriately, to Dr. Bruno that "the lancet, as he well knew, had killed more people than the lance." It was only on April 16, three days before his death, that he at last consented to be bled. According to

Dr. Van Millingen's account he stretched out his arm with the angry words "Come; you are, I see, a damned set of butchers; take away as much blood as you will; but have done with it." This is confirmed exactly in Dr. Bruno's account, who records him as "prestando il braccio in una maniera disgustosa." They then drew a full pound of blood but the fever did not, to their surprise, subside for long. It may well be that, in his then condition, a pound of blood was an excessive quantity to have drawn; but I am assured that in so doing Byron's doctors were in no way violating the conventions of their age. And I doubt whether, even if, as was hoped at one time, an English doctor could have reached him from the garrison at Zante or Corfu, this consultant would have made any very different diagnosis or have prescribed any very different treatment.

The death of Byron was undoubtedly a misfortune, but we should be unfair to Drs. Bruno and Van Millingen were we to perpetuate the legend that it was also an accident.

HAROLD NICOLSON
The Health of Authors
Lancet, 1947.

The Rank and File

In that glittering circle in the firmament, which we call the Galaxie, the milkie-way, there is not one starre of any of the six great magnitudes, which Astronomers proceed upon, belonging to that circle: it is a glorious circle, and possesseth a great part of heaven, and yet is all of so little starres, as have no name, no knowledge taken of them: So certainly there are many . . . not of those great magnitudes, to have been Patriarchs, or Prophets, or Apostles, or Martyrs, or Doctours, or Virgins; but good and blessed souls, that have religiously performed the duties of inferior callings, and no more.

JOHN DONNE
Six Sermons.

Doctor's Wife

A Doctor's Wife writes: "My dear, I never pass a day but I think how lucky you are to have a doctor in the house." . . . So speaks one of the best patients as one is laboriously toiling up the hill with a pram, having abandoned that wretched phone to the fates for an hour. Summer isn't quite so bad, but let me sympathise with all those other poor miserable creatures whose bed-companion is the telephone and whose days are spent keeping food eternally at a reasonable temperature so that the patient may have his doctor. Then, what of the evenings? Mentally and physically exhausted, the evening surgery done, and the last sickly patient tucked safely into bed, home comes the doctor to yet another sliding meal—eight, nine, ten—whatever the whim takes him. The newspaper, a pipe, and after a few minutes loud catarrhal snores. What a cheerful evening! Woe betide the wife who inquires for medical remedies at this juncture; they are doomed to be cast off as mere psychological flights of fancy. Better to keep one's thoughts of aching chilblains or children's spots deep in the crevices of the mind. What is there to it? One often wonders; and still every medical school pours out its numerous doctors, and a thousand crazy females go and land themselves into this heaven, with a doctor "always" in the house.

B.M.J., 1948.

Old Faithful

How shall he become wise that holdeth the plough, that driveth oxen, and is occupied with their labours, and whose talk is of the stock of bulls? He will set his heart upon turning his furrows, and his wakefulness is to give his heifers their fodder. So is every artificer and workmaster that passeth his time by night as by day. . . . So is the smith sitting by the anvil and considering the unwrought iron; in the heat of the furnace will he wrestle with his work, the noise of the hammer will be ever in his ear, and he will set his heart upon making his work perfect. So is the potter sitting at his work and turning the wheel about with his feet. . . .

All these put their trust in their hands, and each becometh wise in his own work. Without these shall not a city be inhabited, and men shall not sojourn nor walk up and down therein. They shall not be found in the council of the people, nor take a high seat in the assembly; they shall not sit on the seat of the judge, nor understand the working of the law courts, nor be found on public platforms. But they will maintain the fabric of the world; and in the handiwork of their craft is their prayer.

Ecclesiasticus, xxxviii.

IV

THE DOCTOR'S WORKSHOP

Three Principles

Not to take authority when I can have facts; not to guess when I can know; not to think a man must take physic because he is sick.   OLIVER WENDELL HOLMES

The Complete Practitioner

This body must be your study, and your continual care—your active, willing, earnest care. Nothing must make you shrink from it. In its weakness and infirmities, in the dishonours of its corruption, you must still value it—still stay by it—to mark its hunger and thirst, its sleeping and waking, its heat and cold; to hear its complaints, to register its groans.

And is it possible to feel an interest in all this? Ay, indeed it is; a greater, far greater, interest than ever a painter or sculptor took in the form and beauties of its health.

Whence comes this interest? At first, perhaps, it seldom comes naturally: a mere sense of duty must engender it; and still, for a while, a mere sense of duty must keep it alive. Presently, the quick, curious, restless spirit of science enlivens it; and then it becomes an excitement, and then a pleasure, and then the deliberate choice of the mind.

When the interest of attending the sick has reached this point, then arises from it, or has already risen, a ready discernment of diseases, and a skill in the use of remedies. And the skill may exalt the interest, and the interest may improve the skill, until, in process of time, experience forms the consummate practitioner.

But does the interest of attending the sick necessarily stop here? The question may seem strange. If it has led to the readiest discernment, and the highest skill, and formed the consummate practitioner, why need it go further?

But what if humanity shall warm it? Then this interest,

this excitement, this intellectual pleasure, is exalted into a principle, and invested with a moral motive, and passes into the heart. What if it be carried still farther? What if religion should animate it? Why, then happy indeed is that man whose mind, whose moral nature, and whose spiritual being, are all harmoniously engaged in the daily business of his life; with whom the same act has become his own happiness, a dispensation of mercy to his fellow-creatures, and a worship of God.

Such a man any of you may be; but you must begin by learning to stand by the sick bed, and make it your delight.

Dr. PETER MERE LATHAM
Lectures on Clinical Medicine, 1836.

Poor in the Midst of Plenty

Why, then, do not we, so rich in preparatory knowledge, so rich in means of diagnosis, produce such men as Baillie, Sydenham, Torti and Stoll? . . . We see that our predecessors, less rich than we are in available knowledge, ceaselessly laboured to originate: poor they were, but they turned to account the tiny stock of information which chance or experience had given them; they exercised their intellectual powers as constantly as wrestlers exercise their muscles, and the result was power, which sometimes showed itself in singular aberrations, but likewise also in views full of greatness and fertility. The very poverty of means increased the intellectual efforts, and the results were immense; and you, surrounded by profusion of means, spoiled, enervated, cloyed with the abundance presented to you, know only how to receive and gorge, while your lazy intellects are smothered with obesity, and are sterile.

For mercy's sake, gentlemen, let us have a little less science, and a little more art! TROUSSEAU
Lectures on Clinical Medicine.

[102]

Doctor and Patient

Every patient, he said, provided two questions—firstly what can be learnt from him and secondly what can be done for him. HARVEY CUSHING

Why do Doctors Make Mistakes?

Why do doctors so often make mistakes? Because they are not sufficiently individual in their diagnosis or their treatment. They class a sick man under some given department of their nosology, whereas every invalid is really a special case, a unique example. How is it possible that so coarse a method of sifting should produce judicious therapeutics? Every illness is a factor simple or complex, which is multiplied by a second factor, invariably complex—the individual, that is to say, who is suffering from it, so that the result is a special problem demanding a special solution, the more so the greater the remoteness of the patient from childhood or from country life.

The principal grievance which I have against the doctors is that they neglect the real problem, which is to seize the unity of the individual who claims their care. Their methods of investigation are much too elementary; a doctor who does not read you to the bottom is ignorant of essentials. To me the ideal doctor would be a man endowed with profound knowledge of life and of the soul, intuitively divining any suffering or disorder of whatever kind, and restoring peace by his mere presence. Such a doctor is possible, but the greater of them lack the higher and inner life, they know nothing of the transcendent laboratories of nature: they seem to me superficial, profane, strangers to divine things, destitute of intuition and sympathy. The model doctor should be at once a genius, a saint, a man of God.

H. F. AMIEL
Journal Intime

The Consultation

You will remember, of course, always to get the weather-gage of your patient, I mean, to place him so that the light falls on his face and not on yours. It is a kind of ocular duel that is about to take place between you; you are going to look through his features into his pulmonary and hepatic and other internal machinery, and he is going to look into yours quite as sharply to see what you think about his probabilities for time and eternity.

OLIVER WENDELL HOLMES

Surgery the Salvation of Medicine

From the time of Hippocrates surgery has ever been the salvation of inner medicine. In inner medicine physicians have dwelt too much in dogmas, opinions and speculations; and too often their errors passed undiscovered to the grave. The surgeon, for his good, has had a sharper training on facts; his errors hit him promptly in the face.

Sir CLIFFORD ALLBUTT
Lancet, 1922.

Taking a History

The best memory is a record made at the time.

Sir WILLIAM GULL
Aphorisms.

I will set down what comes from her to satisfy my remembrance the more strongly.

WILLIAM SHAKESPEARE
Macbeth.

[104]

What Makes a Great Physician?

I would answer that *he is a great physician who, above other men, understands diagnosis.* It is not he who promises to cure all maladies, who has a remedy ready for every symptom, or one remedy for all symptoms; who boasts that success never fails him, when his daily history gives the lie to such assertion. It is rather he, who, with just discrimination, looks at a case in all its difficulties; who to habits of correct reasoning, adds the acquirements obtained from study and observation; who is trustworthy in common things for his common sense, and in professional things for his judgment, learning and experience; who forms his opinion positive or approximative, according to the evidence; who looks at the necessary results of inevitable causes; who promptly does what man may do of good, and carefully avoids what he may do of evil.

Dr. JACOB BIGELOW
Nature in Disease, 1852.

Father Confessor

Hannah More wondered why people should be so fond of the company of their physician till she recollected that he was the only person with whom one dared to talk continually of oneself, without interruption, contradiction or censure.

Sir ROBERT HUTCHISON
B.M.J., 1934.

Listen to the Patient

The most important difference between a good and indifferent clinician lies in the amount of attention paid to the story of a patient.

Sir FARQUHAR BUZZARD
Lancet, 1933.

Of Right Observation

The power of correct observation is not the attribute of ignorance, but is *ceteris paribus*, always proportionate to the knowledge the individual possesses. With what additional profit and success does the painter, the sculptor, the naturalist, observe after a long cultivation of their respective arts, and how numerous are the details detected which would wholly escape the unpractised novice? Now if an accurate conception of external characters, when passive under the eye of the observer, demands long and patient exercise for its acquirement, how much greater must be the difficulties surrounding the complicated machine of the human frame, under all the varied influences and the innumerable modifications of which it is susceptible? The phenomena are not only complex and ever varying, but they must often be examined through the distorting medium of a suffering and fanciful mind, and are frequently described with the intention to mislead and deceive.

Dr. CHARLES COWAN
Translator's Introduction to Louis' Phthisis, 1835.

Beware of Hurry

The credit of physicians and physic would be every day more and more established if they were not too apt to precipitate their opinions. It is well, when a physician can be able to say to himself, "I have never been in too great a hurry."

Dr. ZIMMERMANN
A Treatise on Experience in Physic, 1782.

The Confidence of Patients

Most patients long for someone to whom they can confide their troubles. For this they look to the doctor, and it makes little difference whether he is clerk, interne or practitioner so long as he is the right sort. It may only be necessary for students to have recourse to a simple conversation; to show real interest in this man or that woman, as an individual, in order to let loose a flood of startling confidences. At other times, the way is not so clear, suspicions and fears must be allayed before the friendly relation can be established. And then there comes, little by little, or sometimes in torrents, a more or less disjointed story, which, when pieced together, gives the record of a human life surprisingly valuable, at times, in disclosing an explanation for the actual physical ailment. You thus increase your knowledge of human nature, often learn a way to help the patient in his distress, and in addition gain a friend.

WARFIELD T. LONGCOPE
Methods and Medicine
Bull. Johns Hopkins Hospital, 1932.

Having Eyes, They See Not

The trouble with doctors is not that they don't know enough, but that they don't see enough.

Sir DOMINIC J. CORRIGAN, 1853.

Examining the Patient

It is an art to secure a complete and accurate history of a patient's sickness. While subject to the laws of logic, securing the history of the patient is much the same as cross-examination of a witness by an acute lawyer. And the physical examination is wholly an art. The accuracy of the observations made depends entirely upon the technical proficiency of the physician. Knowledge of the significance of physical signs alone is useless unless it be combined with the technical expertness to detect these signs. There is a close analogy between clinical medicine and music. One may know harmony, counterpoint, and all that makes up the science of music, but unless by dint of practice he has mastered technique there will be no music. Technique in music produces beauty of tone; in medicine it secures accuracy of data. There are many sources of error in diagnosis, errors in data, but the commonest of all are errors of technique.

Diagnosis is then a science and an art; a science in the method of using facts secured, an art largely in the mode of collecting facts.

Dr. NELLIS B. FOSTER
The Examination of Patients.

Anamnesis

To conduct this cross-questioning correctly, in such a manner, so to speak, that it quickly attains its object—the correct diagnosis—is an art which must not be undervalued, for it is here that the skilful physician's ability intrinsically reveals itself. Naturally a thorough knowledge of pathological anatomy is essential, for without this you are not in a position to appreciate the many possibilities which will present themselves. Imagination, presence of mind, criticism, and the gift of logical combination are next called for, though perhaps psychological perceptivity, self-control, and a sense of superiority among human beings are even more important.

You will quickly learn that all patients will not allow themselves to be measured with the same rule. If you wish to learn anything useful from your patients, you must take each in his own particular way. A patient is lively, talkative, imaginative, and speaks fast and loose of all sorts of things at full speed, but seldom remembers to mention that upon which everything depends. Here you must apply the brake as quickly as possible, and ask short precise questions, while insisting upon short precise answers; else he breaks away from your examination, and all his remarks become immaterial. Another patient may be reticent and distrustful, so that his evidence has to be hauled forth. But the very greatest drawback with patients is, that so many of them are anxious and nervous, partly from fear of illness, partly from fear of the physician, and of what he will do to them. From these patients you will not obtain a sensible word if you meet them with a serious, solemn face, or if you yourself appear nervous and anxious. You must first soothe them with a kindly and cheerful address, and if you are capable of making a little joke or a humorous remark you will often have the good fortune immediately to make them calm and confident.

On the whole, you must remember, when associating with the sick, that these require kindness most of all, and that they first and foremost wish and hope to find a comprehending and sympathetic friend in their physician; and when treated in this manner will, in a few moments, give you their fullest confidence.

THORKILD ROVSING
Clinical Lectures on Abdominal Surgery.

What Every Patient Wants

There are four questions which in some form or other every patient asks his doctor:

(*a*) What is the matter with me? This is *diagnosis*.

(*b*) Can you put me right? This is *treatment* and *prognosis*.

(*c*) How did I get it? This is *causation*.

(*e*) How can I avoid it in future? This is *prevention*.

. . . He may not be called upon to attempt a full answer to his patient, but he must give a fair working answer to himself.

Sir GEORGE NEWMAN
Preventive Medicine for the Medical Student
Lancet, 1931.

Of Judgment in Diagnosis

Every doctor must be a judge. He has to weigh the evidence of symptoms and signs, and allot to each its proper value in making the diagnosis. Now we have Hippocratic authority for the belief that "judgment is difficult," and, indeed, medicine has been defined as "the art of coming to a conclusion on insufficient evidence," so it need be no matter for surprise that errors of judgment so often lead to erroneous diagnosis.

We can increase our powers of observation by training and practice, and we can extend their range by means of special instruments and methods. We can increase our knowledge by study and experience, but can we improve our powers of judgment? I greatly doubt it. Judgment seems to be an inborn faculty, the result of a union of mind and character, which a man either has or has not, and it is almost as difficult for him to increase it as to add a cubit to his stature. . . .

What is sometimes called "clinical instinct" is, in truth, simply a power of rapid instinctive judgment, and it may be lacking in men of high intellectual ability and present to a marked degree in those who are in other respects mentally their inferiors. It seems to be much the same as "common sense" and closely allied to a sense of humour, which is the same thing as a sense of proportion. Those who lack it are apt, in making a diagnosis, to fail to see the wood for the trees.

If the natural powers of judgment are to be improved it is only, I believe, by general mental culture, and not by purely scientific training, that it can be done. The study of "humanism," by which is meant the philosophy of knowledge as opposed to its practical application, must be the means. As someone has said, sanity, humour, breadth of view, and powers of criticism are the distinguishing marks of the humanist, and it is at these that we must aim. It is for this reason that I regret the modern tendency to make the scientific studies of the medical student begin at an earlier age and whilst he is still at school, and to sacrifice to them much of the old literary and linguistic training. It is, I think, not without significance in this regard that many of the most distinguished physicians of the last generation have also been good classical scholars.

Sir ROBERT HUTCHISON
The Principles of Diagnosis
B.M.J., 1928.

Diagnosis is not Enough

Young doctors are particularly strong on what they call *diagnosis*—an excellent branch of the healing art, full of satisfaction to the curious practitioner who likes to give the right Latin name to one's complaints; not quite so satisfactory to the patient, as it is not so very much pleasanter to be bitten by a dog with a collar round his neck telling you that he is called *Snap* or *Teaser*, than by a dog without a collar. Sometimes, in fact, one would a little rather not know the exact name of his complaint, as if he does he is pretty sure to look it out in a medical dictionary, and then if he reads "This terrible disease is attended with vast suffering and is inevitably mortal," or any such statement, it is apt to affect him unpleasantly.

OLIVER WENDELL HOLMES
The Poet at the Breakfast Table.

Clinical Sense

One of the Guy's surgeons had a case of ununited fracture which was giving him concern, and decided one day with his house surgeon to waylay Sir William Gull and ask his advice on the case, scarcely expecting that he would have any useful contribution to make to so surgical a problem. Gull took a look at the man and said "Feed him on tomatoes" —nothing more. The instruction was obeyed and the fracture united. When asked later by the surgeon his reasons for this advice, he replied that the surgeon and his house-surgeon might know all about fractures but had failed to observe that the man had signs of scurvy.

J. A. RYLE
Clinical Sense and Clinical Science
Lancet, 1939.

Time the Preceptor

"Euriphon the Physician, being asked what preceptor had the teaching of him, made answer that his preceptor was Time." These words are quoted by Dr. Heberden and stand the last of his "Commentary on the History and Cure of Diseases. . . ."

And time keeps school among physicians still. But he is not, and never was, a popular lecturer. He is slow in coming to the point. He has a cautious, hesitating, self-correcting manner, which is not altogether pleasant, and makes him difficult to follow. Hence a good deal more patience is required to understand his teaching, and profit by it, than most men care to give. That his disciples should value highly what their venerable preceptor has hammered into them is natural enough. But then they are themselves few and grey-headed, and have often caught something of their master's manner, and so do not obtain a ready ear from the world.

Dr. PETER MERE LATHAM
Lectures on Clinical Medicine, 1836.

Of the Doctor's Errors

It may be granted freely that a bad diagnosis due to an error of judgment is more excusable than one attributable to want of knowledge or even to faulty observation. The ghosts of dead patients which at the midnight hour haunt the bedside of every doctor who has been some years in practice will not upbraid him with such questions as "Why did you not know that a ball-valve gall stone may produce symptoms like those of malaria?" or still less "Why did you not attach more importance to the rapidity of my pulse, and less to the signs in my abdomen?" No; the unescapable questions

H   [113]

they will put to him will be such as these: "Why did you not examine my fundi for optic neuritis?" or "Why did you not put a finger in my rectum?"

Sir ROBERT HUTCHISON
The Principles of Diagnosis
B.M.J., 1928.

Clinical Instinct

The valuable property of "clinical instinct," which although sometimes ridiculed as the assumed armour and decoration of the ignoramus or the quack, has a certain resemblance to the poetic faculty, and moreover is a real asset in practice. Clinical instinct is the power of arriving without a conscious logical process at a definite conclusion, and is often possessed in a high degree by old nurses who know, but cannot give their reasons, whether a patient is going to recover or die, and by practitioners of long experience who similarly cannot explain the steps by which they reach a diagnosis and prognosis. It may be assumed that they unwittingly draw on a buried experience which, without their conscious remembrance, recognises in the patient signs presented by one in the long past. In diagnosis, therefore, there are the two processes—the consciously logical, and the rarer, but not necessarily less correct, the unconscious.

Sir HUMPHRY ROLLESTON
Poetry and Physic
B.M.J., 1925.

Diagnosis by Intuition

Diagnosis by intuition is a rapid method of reaching a wrong conclusion.

JOHN CHALMERS DA COSTA
Selected Papers and Speeches, 1931.

The Science of Diagnosis

The science of diagnosis is, in the main, a science of observation, the aim of which is to detect in the living patient processes and lesions which are beyond our reach, but which would, in most instances, be revealed at a *post-mortem* examination. Yet it rests largely upon *post-mortem* teachings, and all who aim at becoming capable diagnosticians should take advantage of every opportunity afforded to them of seeing and whenever possible conducting, such examinations. Such opportunities are most common during student days, and only too many of us regret in after life the neglect of such opportunities; for morbid anatomy, one of the most important subjects in the medical curriculum, can only be learnt by personal observation. Do not forget that there is an immense difference between facts which we *know* and facts with which we are merely acquainted. Facts which we know are not those about which we have read, or have heard in lectures, but those which we have observed, apprehended, and confirmed for ourselves. We need no *memoria technica* to recall a fact which we *know*.

Sir ARCHIBALD GARROD
B.M.J., 1926.

Lay Your Foundations Well

All this new and precious technique supplements, it does not supplant, the fundamental procedures of observation and physical examination of which Laënnec and Bright made use. We must not forget that a thorough training in the fundamental art of physical exploration is as vital as ever, that the necessary period of experience spent at the bedside of the patient has not been shortened by a day. Familiarity with the symptoms of disease, an ability to recognise and interpret these symptoms—which may be obtained only by experience—are among the first requisites for him who would be a competent physician. No amount of learning can supply this familiarity, this ability. The intelligent interpretation of symptoms is the first step. He who has not seen the development of progress of disease, he who has not followed the affected subject to his recovery or to his death, he who has not seen his diagnosis confirmed again and again after death, will never attain this familiarity; he will be unfit to practise much less to teach the art of medicine.

W. S. THAYER
B.M.J., 1927.

Dont's for Diagnosticians

1. Don't be too clever.

2. Don't diagnose rarities.

3. Don't be in a hurry.

4. Don't be faddy.

5. Don't mistake a label for a diagnosis.

6. Don't diagnose two diseases simultaneously in the same patient.

7. Don't be too cock-sure.

8. Don't be biassed.

9. Don't hesitate to revise your diagnosis from time to time in a chronic case.

Sir ROBERT HUTCHISON
The Principles of Diagnosis
B.M.J., 1928.

Diagnosis as Detection

It is tempting to compare the methods of diagnosis with those of crime detection: (i) a criminal may be caught in the act—the pediculi responsible for scalp infections and the threadworms for pruritis ani; or (ii) there may be obvious clues, such as the facies of acromegaly and jaundice; or (iii) clues might be obtained only after careful searching by the ordinary methods of examination or by means of extended perception given us by instruments of precision, for example, in an abdominal aneurysm, or in a pleural effusion. In nearly all cases the solution to the diagnostic problem is suggested by the history. It provides the circumstantial evidence. For example, in biliary colic, where there might be no observable abnormal signs on examination except those subsequently unmasked by accessory measures, we are led straight from the history to these necessary and crucial tests. There is one word of warning which applies to physicians whatever the nature of their practice or specialty. It is that no observation however small or apparently trivial, which fails to fit into the tentative diagnosis, should be put on one side as unimportant. As the famous detective Hercule Poirot, in Agatha Christie's novel *The Mysterious Affair at Styles*, said, "Beware! peril to the detective who says 'it is so small—it does not matter. It will not agree. I will forget it.' That way lies confusion—everything matters!"

Sir HENRY COHEN
The Nature, Method and Purpose of Diagnosis.

The Stuff of Divinity

We touch heaven when we lay our hand on a human body.

NORVALIS

The Pre-Harveian Physician

There is nothing more difficult for us moderns than to feel a pulse with the finger of a pre-Harveian physician. Under his finger the artery expanded of itself, drawing in blood, spirits, air and vapours of all sorts and squeezing them out again as it contracted. We feel only Harvey's stroke of the heart—the arteries distending as "when a bladder is filled." We see the patient's body as a great capillary field, uniting arteries and veins—a field of whose existence Harvey knew nothing save by inference. We think in terms of oxygen, carbon dioxide, and combustion; even Harvey had to content himself with "vital spirits," "fuliginous vapours" and "innate heat." To the pre-Harveian physician the human body was a realm dominated by a cosmogony of spirits. Harvey's greatest service to medicine was not the discovery of the circulation, but his rescue of medicine from the demonology of myth.

Sir ARTHUR KEITH
Harvey as Anatomist
Lancet, 1928.

On the Art of Feeling

Let me lay down this one fundamental rule: "Feel with a light, soft touch," not only in order to cause the patient as little distress and pain as possible, but because the more lightly and tentatively you use your hands, the more surely and delicately you feel. A hard and coarse hand never arrives at a delicate diagnosis.

THORKILD ROVSING
Clinical Lectures on Abdominal Surgery.

Study the Normal

Neglect of a proper study of healthy signs is the secret of the failure of many who undertake to master auscultation and percussion.

AUSTIN FLINT, 1881.

The Harassed Student Might Well Agree

Dr. James Arthur Wilson, physician to St. George's Hospital from 1829 to 1857, who from his initials JAW signed anonymous articles "Maxilla," is recorded by his son-in-law W. H. Dickinson to have remarked after listening to a case of bronchopneumonia, "Strange sounds, strange sounds."

St. George's Hospital Gazette.

An Old Gibe

By means of an instrument called the stethoscope, applied to the breast bone, some modern medical writers profess to discover what is going on within. This new art is called auscultation, and the internal sounds pectoriloquism. By means of this new discovery a learned physician professes to have heard a "metallic tinkling" at the heart or in the lungs of a patient. A bystander, however, thinks the "metallic tinkling" was only audible from two pieces of coin which found their way into the palm of the doctor.

Observer, April 1830
(11 years after the appearance of Laënnec's classical work).

Of Mistakes

Cet enrichement de nos connaissances ainsi acquis, grâce à une erreur de diagnostic, ne va pas sans une certaine amertume, si utiles que soient les leçons que cela puisse nous donner pour l'avenir. . . .

On ne sera jamais *assez* minutieux dans l'examen objectif du malade, mais il faudra se garder d'être *trop* subtil dans les conclusions qu'on tire des découvertes objectives.

CHRISTIANSSEN
Tumeurs du Cerveau.

Of Diagnosis by Signs

There are two sorts of error in diagnosis by signs—one negative, the other positive. Negative errors are perhaps commonest, and arise from overlooking signs which are present; they are chiefly made by those ill trained in clinical methods. Positive errors consist in detecting signs which have no real existence—the discovery, in short, of mares' nests. They are chiefly made by those with observational zeal, but little knowledge or experience. The apex of the right lung, the pulmonary area of the heart, and the right iliac fossa are the regions in which mares' nests are specially common.

Sir ROBERT HUTCHISON
The Principles of Diagnosis
B.M.J., 1928.

Of the Stethoscope

Books and essays without number, and of great value, have been written for the purpose of adding favourable testimony to the merits of the stethoscope: to increase its utility, and extend its application; whereas, so far as I know, not a single individual has deemed it right or desirable to pursue the opposite course, of expressly publishing to the world the manifold difficulties and fallacies attending its use. The publications alluded to, by the semblance of a too exclusive advocacy, have, according to my humble belief, placed the stethoscope and its pretensions in a false position; they have awakened in the minds of many a vague notion of infallibility; they have led the profession and the public to expect too much, and by suppressing or concealing the real parties to inculpate the stethoscope for the errors of the stethoscopist. But if the works of even able and experienced writers have thus done injury to the cause of physical diagnosis, and have furnished weapons of attack to its opponents; what shall we say of that very numerous class of persons who, with the most slender experience, mistake zeal for proficiency, and are perpetually falling into grievous and palpable error? The enthusiasm, the rashness, the bigotry and conceit of the exclusive stethoscopist have indeed most seriously retarded the adoption, and vitiated the claims of physical diagnosis; and have done more to discourage the student, to shake the confidence of the profession, and to throw ridicule upon the stethoscope itself than the most inveterate hostility could ever have accomplished. They seem to look upon the instrument as all-sufficient; they rush at once to auscultation and percussion; they neglect or disdain to make those careful and minute inquiries which no sound and sensible physician ever fails to do, and thereby convert an invaluable auxiliary into what, in their hands at least, proves but an imperfect and treacherous substitute.

THOMAS ADDISON
The Difficulties and Fallacies attending Physical Diagnosis in Diseases of the Chest, 1846.

Priorities

In surgery, eyes first and most: fingers next and little; tongue last and least.

Sir GEORGE MURRAY HUMPHRY

Common Sense

Common sense is in medicine the master workman. With it a few good solid materials become the ways and means to practical results infinitely various and important; without it, materials ever so many and ever so good come to nothing or come to mischief.

Dr. PETER MERE LATHAM
Lectures on Clinical Medicine, 1836.

Mind What You Say

A young man went to a doctor for a life insurance examination. The doctor took his pulse and tested his heart and in doing so looked at his watch, shook his head, and said, "Dear, dear!" The patient was perfectly convinced that this was his death sentence, and his mournful reflections on it so turned his mind that eventually he came under the care of a psychiatrist. The psychiatrist investigated the matter and, knowing the insurance examiner, rang him up and asked what was organically wrong with this young man. "Sound as a bell," was the reply. "But he says," the other went on, "that when you examined him you looked at your watch, shook your head, and said, 'Dear, dear!'" The doctor reflected a moment and then said, "So I did. I looked at my watch and found the darned thing had stopped again."

B.M.J., 1947.

Of the Use of Instruments of Precision

It is not at first sight obvious how the use of instruments of precision and the insistence on precise methods in their use favours the establishment of truthfulness as a corner stone of our dealings with each other and with our patients. But although this is not obvious, I am convinced that it is true. Anyone who records his cases and makes his observations in an inaccurate and slovenly way, finds his mind filled with a kind of haze. To clear away this haze when he comes to state his results, it is almost inevitable that he should fall into the habit of drawing upon sources other than reality for his materials and for his terms. If, on the other hand, a man has made his analyses, his measurements, and his clinical records accurately and thoroughly, he learns to *lean upon facts*, and to have confidence that whatever is true will turn out to work well. Thus he gets out of the habit of improvising, modifying or embellishing his statements to suit traditional or preconceived ideas. . . .

I know no form of labour which the average man shuns more instinctively and more constantly than the labour of thinking or of fresh observation. But the doctor is human and capable of temptation all the more readily when the tempter assumes the subtle and baffling guise of the "scientific method." I know a doctor who never forgets his stethoscope, his blood counter or his percussion hammer when he starts on his rounds in the morning, yet not infrequently he is so absent-minded as to leave at home one all-important instrument—his brain. . . .

R. C. CABOT
The Ideal of Accuracy in Clinical Work
Boston M. and S. Journal, 1904.

"Shadows not Substantial Things"

"Doctor," said a patient to me, "I hope you will be different from the many physicians whom I have consulted. I hope you will examine the x-ray films less and me more."

Dr. HERRICK

Prognosis

A physician should not be forward to make gloomy prognostications; because they savour of empiricism, by magnifying the importance of his services in the treatment or cure of the disease. But he should not fail, on proper occasions, to give to the friends of the patient timely notice of danger when it really occurs, and even to the patient himself, if absolutely necessary.   Dr. THOMAS PERCIVAL

Medical Ethics, 1803.

Body and Mind

A man's body and his mind, with the utmost reverence to both I speak it, are exactly like a jerkin, and a jerkin's lining; rumple the one, you rumple the other.

STERNE, Life and Opinions of Tristram Shandy.

Hope

A successful physician once told me that he never left a house without giving a favourable prognosis; a counsel which had perhaps a colour of worldly wisdom about it; but this far he was right—that we cannot foresee what benediction words of hope may bestow. I have told a story elsewhere of one who asked his doctor what boon he supposed to be most desired of him by his patients. Was it diagnosis, or medicines, or skill, or kindly counsel? No! none of these was the most precious: what the patient yearned for, the remedy to put the most heart into him, was Hope. *Vivere spe vidi qui moriturus erat.*

Sir CLIFFORD ALLBUTT
Lancet, 1922.

The Sources of Quackery

It was a favourite saying of Dr. Cullen, that there are in physick more false facts than false theories. It is by the want of due caution with regard to the former that quackery has chiefly been sustained. For those who do not belong to the profession, being off their guard, from not being in the habit of observing and reflecting on the fallacy of testimony and other sources of error; and being eager to catch at relief from whatever quarter, perhaps with minds soured by disappointment, and exquisitively sensitive to hopes and fears however vain, become sanguine and credulous on the slightest prospect of relief. These impressions are also wonderfully favoured by the operation of mystery and concealment; for there is a peculiar interest and importance attached to whatever is secret. *Il y a quelque chose de singulièrement piquant dans le mystère*, says some French author. It is difficult to explain this, but it seems to be an emanation of the same principle in human nature, as the *ignotum pro magnifico* of the poet. The credit of these remedies is also greatly enhanced by the successful cases only being made public; for the innumerable cases in which they are used, whether openly or secretly, without the boasted good effects, still more, if with bad effects, are never reported; while those supposed to be successful are studiously promulgated. And there is here a farther source of false or dubious testimony; for those who are induced to use these remedies, being anxious to ward off reproach or derision, justify themselves by making the most favourable report, and even by affecting to have received relief: and not frequently fancying and honestly believing that they have actually received it.

Sir GILBERT BLANE
Elements of Medical Logick, 1825.

Barren Enthusiasms

There is no doubt of the fact that what may be taken up to-day without reason or proof by a plausible enthusiast or two will have the multitude of the profession using, and believing in, and swearing by, a few months hence; and thus it will gain a credit from which the contrary experience and sober dissent of well-judging minds will never be able to set us free. Unfortunately, where there is no experiment of exact science to settle the matter, it takes as much time and trouble to pull down a falsehood as to build up a truth. Only let the most worthless nostrum get backed by the credit of some good name, and it will never cease to pass current for something in the world, and will never be altogether got rid of from our materia medica. Thus, upon the whole, it is sad to think how much of the practice of medicine is blindly engaged in a busy, noisy workshop of impossibilities.

Dr. PETER MERE LATHAM
Lectures on Clinical Medicine, 1836.

Deceptions in Medicine

Deceptions in medicine are occasioned not only by the dishonesty of charlatans, but quite as often by the well-meaning credulity of other practitioners, whose intellect is impulsive, or whose education has been unduly curtailed. It is so flattering to a man's self-love to believe that his chance shots have sometimes taken effect, that physicians of regular position may pass their lives in mere speculation and random efforts at curing diseases, shutting their eyes against their own failures, and not allowing themselves to consider that in a certain portion of successful cases which they had failed to understand, the disease in truth got well without, or perhaps in spite of, their misdirected and embarrassing practice.

[126]

Medicine is a great good and unquestionable blessing to mankind, when it is administered by discriminating and intelligent hands with sincerity and good judgment. It disappoints expectation, and fails to accomplish its mission when the agent who dispenses it falls into the mistaken resource of professing infallibility, and of raising hopes which he knows not how to accomplish. No man is deemed to be safe in his worldly affairs who is afraid to look into his own pecuniary condition. Neither is a physician safe in his practice or his reputation who is afraid to face the case of his patient in all its bearings. That man is most to be relied upon who looks calmly and understandingly at the emergency before him, who knows the import of the signs, and deduces from them the probable tenor of coming events; who is aware of the great truth that all men must die, but is also aware of the more gratifying truth that most sick men recover; and who, in particular exigencies, inquires of his reason and knowledge, in which of these two immediate categories his patient is placed, and how far the event of the case is within his control. He will then interfere or he will wait, he will act or he will forbear, as he only knows how who can form a correct verdict from the evidence before him, and knows the immeasurable good or harm which hangs on medical practice.

Dr. Jacob Bigelow
Nature in Disease, 1852.

Quackery

It is commonly said that education is a great safeguard against quackery and faddery. I profoundly disbelieve it. So far as I can see, the higher one goes in the social scale, the more does fashion in health matters prevail, and the so-called *intelligentsia* are the most gullible of all.

Sir Robert Hutchison
B.M.J., 1934.

How to Become a Charlatan

If you are determined to become a charlatan, the first thing to do is to take full advantage of the present taste for obscurity in expression and of contemporary leniency towards unsupported assertions. You will by that means avoid exposing your incapacity for thought and the meagreness of your knowledge. Thus what would otherwise be serious drawbacks may actually become advantages. And on no account neglect to pepper your writings with jibes at the inadequacy of reason and assertions about the trustworthiness of instinct. With regard to your personal behaviour, which is so important in the career of a charlatan, I have very few suggestions to offer, but be careful only to praise a competitor whom you have obviously surpassed, and then, *most* emphatically, for the least of his talents. This will give others a high opinion of your generosity and at the same time do him very little good. And if you praise yourself, which you must do from time to time, adopt a plaintive and indignant tone as if you had been forced to do it by the injustice of the world. Boast frequently in talking to women, but in talking to men content yourself as a rule with speaking in carelessly disparaging tones of great men and great work. Also when you attack your enemies, attack them *en bloc*; this has an air of courage while it is far less dangerous than attacking individuals. In choosing subjects select, if possible, those on which better men than you have, after much research and thought, failed to reach a conclusion. Such subjects will supply you with hopeful readers, and spare you the toil of original enquiry. Where evidence for your assertions is wholly lacking, a generous but discrete use of the words "of course" is to be recommended.

"AFFABLE HAWK" (now Sir DESMOND MACCARTHY), in the *New Statesman*.

[128]

False Remedies

When remedies claiming however falsely a special curative power, have been long in use, it is almost impossible ever to get rid of them. Their use then becomes a good deal like what the game of shuttlecock would be played by a crowd. The shuttlecock need never fall to the ground; there are so many to knock it about and keep it up. But, on such terms, it is a stupid game, or rather no game at all, and any left-handed clown can play at it.

Dr. Peter Mere Latham
Lectures on Clinical Medicine, 1836.

Fashionable Doctor

Still, one should not envy the fashionable doctor; rather one should wonder at him. He leads a life of slavery even although, as a wag said, it is slavery on the Guinea coast, and circumstanced as he is, good and thorough work becomes impossible. His position, too, on a pinnacle is always precarious. He has, it is true, his little day, but he is apt to wake up one morning to find that his worshippers have stampeded *en masse* overnight to some newer shrines of the fickle goddess Fashion.

Sir Robert Hutchison
B.M.J., 1934.

" They Also Serve "

It is a great mistake to suppose that Nature always stands in need of the assistance of Art . . . nor do I think it below me to acknowledge that, when no manifest indication pointed out to me what was to be done, I have consulted the safety of my patient and my own reputation effectually by doing nothing at all.

Sydenham

I

The Quack—and the Goose

The quack has a considerable advantage over the regular practitioner. If any one of his promises becomes realised, he is applauded to the skies; and if the patient finds himself deceived, he is obliged in honour to be silent, that he may not expose himself to blame for having confided himself to a wretch who has the more right to deceive as the number of simple people is always the greatest. Besides, this daring man risks no loss of reputation; because as it exists only amongst ignorant people, the blame will always incline towards those who have listened to him. Men are so fond of the marvellous that the quack has above all others the power of making the vulgar relish novelty. The more absurd his promises are, the more he is attended to. He applies a barbarous name to a plant he has just gathered at the entrance of the village, and then giving the details of his miracles, this plant is adopted for the cure of every infirmity.

Dr. ZIMMERMANN
A Treatise on Experience in Physic, 1782.

" Je le pansay, Dieu le guérit "

Among well-educated physicians the word *cure*, as applied to their own merits, is proscribed as presumptuous, and rarely, I believe, escapes the lips of any practitioner whose mind is duly tinctured with that ingenuous modesty which characterises the liberal and correct members of the profession.

Sir GILBERT BLANE
Elements of Medical Logick, 1825.

Of Credulity

Credulity may be less unamiable than scepticism; we may be disposed to regard the former as an infirmity untainted by selfishness, whilst we look upon the latter as too often blended with envy, hatred, or malice; still they are alike opposed to the advancement of truth. In the present instance, indeed, the man of science may be permitted to dissent from the moralist; since scepticism, whatever shape it may assume, or from whatever motives it may proceed, serves but to provoke discussion, to encourage inquiry, and to subject all novel pretensions to the searching test of repeated and careful experiment; whereas the tendency of an easy belief is just as certainly to create and strengthen prejudice, to engender misguided enthusiasm, and to pervert or suspend the exercise of that calmer judgment so essential to the honest and impartial investigation of facts.

> THOMAS ADDISON
> *The Difficulties and Fallacies attending Physical Diagnosis in Diseases of the Chest*, 1846.

The Mind in Therapeutics

I remember an ingenious physician who told me in the fanatic times he found most of his patients so disturbed by troubles of conscience that he was forced to play the divine with them before he could begin the physician: whose greatest skill perhaps also lies in the infusing of hopes, and inducing some composure and tranquillity of mind before they enter upon the other operations of their art.

> Sir WILLIAM TEMPLE, 1628-1699
> *Of Health and Long Life*.

The Magic of the Bottle of Medicine

Our experiments with the ergograph were made on healthy men under a regular regime. . . . We found that a dose of caffeine dissolved in water one hour before the experiment greatly increased the output of work for that day. This was repeated on several occasions, always with the same result and we naturally regarded the effect as due to the caffeine. This, however, was not the case: the effect was due to the ritual of taking a drug; the drug day assumed an enhanced importance in the mind of the operator and the mental effect sometimes referred to as suggestion was principally responsible. We had no difficulty in showing that water made bitter with a trace of quassia or other simple bitter had a similar effect.

Prof. W. E. DIXON
Physiology—the basis of treatment
Lancet, 1929.

The One Thing More

God works by means, as Christ cured the blind man with clay and spittle. *Orandum est ut sit mens sana in corpore sano.* As we must pray for health of body and mind, so we must use our utmost endeavours to preserve and continue it. Some kind of devils are not cast out but by fasting and prayer, and both necessarily required, not one without the other. For all the physick we can use, art, excellent industry, is to no purpose without calling on God: it is vain to seek for help, run, ride, except God bless us. Hippocrates, an heathen, required this in a good practitioner, and so did Galen.

BURTON
Anatomy of Melancholy, 1561.

[132]

The Treatment of Patients

Every observant practitioner knows that he treats patients rather than diseases. He does not regard the former as the chemist does his crucibles, retorts, and test-glasses, which have no reaction upon their contents, but he knows that every substance taken into the body acts upon it and is itself acted upon by it, and in innumerable modes and degrees, according to the existing condition of the body and the quantity, combination, and form of administration of the medicine; so that there is some ground for the sarcastic comment that "the art of medicine consists in introducing a body of which we know little into another of which we know still less."

It is quite as necessary for the physician to know when to abstain from the use of medicines as it is for him to prescribe when medication is necessary; that he must, as far as possible, see the end of a disease from its beginning; that he must never forget that medical art has a far higher range and aim than the prescription of drugs, or even of food and hygienic means; and that when neither of these avails to ward off the fatal ending, it is still no small portion of his art to rid his patient's path of thorns if he cannot make it bloom with roses.

Dr. Alfred Stillé

Good Advice

Eat slowly; only men in rags
And gluttons old in sin
Mistake themselves for carpet bags
And shovel victuals in.

Sir Walter Raleigh
(*Sometime Professor of Poetry at Oxford.*)

[133]

Of Advising Surgical Intervention

The practitioner's responsibility is of a two-fold nature. All practitioners properly feel the responsibility of advising patients to undergo operation, and they all feel this because the fears and many scruples of the patient react upon the mind of the practitioner, while on the other hand, he is far less sensible of responsibility if he refrains from advising surgical assistance in cases of certainty or doubt simply because no one, in either case, would saddle him with the responsibility. No one, that is to say, save his own conscience. This responsibility is, in consequence, often overlooked and forgotten, more is the pity; because, as a matter of fact, it is a greater and more serious responsibility than that incurred by advising surgical counsel, for in the latter case, if interference be not necessary, the fact will be opportunely recognised by the experienced surgeon whose assistance has been sought, and thus no misfortune occurs; while on the other hand, neglect of a timely call for such surgical help, when needed, often results in loss of life. . . . It should always be every good physician's pride, above all things, to preserve the feeling of this responsibility steadily alight and awake in his conscience, and the more so, because in the world's eye, he can so easily avoid it.

THORKILD ROVSING
Clinical Lectures on Abdominal Surgery.

Let Your Yea be Yea

Launched in a country practice, in those days a cross-section of the rural population, I realised that for some years I should have to watch; and try, too, on the hit and miss principle, to find out rules for the guidance in the management of people of varied habits. A story my predecessor told me, convinced me of the need for definite bases for the advice I gave. He had been called to the Squire on account of gout, and had ordered fish. He had hardly reached home when a groom rode up with a note. "Dear Sir, boiled fish or fried? Yr. obedt. Servt. . . ." What he replied does not concern us here; but I was impressed by the old doctor's advice to be precise in dietetic directions.

Dr. L. J. PICTON
Liverpool Medico-Chirurgical Journal, 1931.

Mistaken Pride

The humility which we may learn from the limited influence of our art on the health and lives of mankind, is probably a far safer guide to a correct practice than the fanatical confidence with which unenlightened ultraists of every sect carry out their respective dogmas. In a sphere of action where some good may always be done, and where much harm often is done, and "fools rush in where angels fear to tread," it is well to consider some of the rules which may lead an honest inquirer after truth to the nearest attainment to a correct judgment and practice. . . . It often happens that the nature of the case cannot be made out in one, or two, or three interviews with the patient, and we are obliged to wait for the gradual development of diagnostic symptoms, as a judge and jury in a like case would be expected to postpone, or wait for the arrival of witnesses. It is a mistaken pride which leads physicians to commit themselves by an oracular guess at first sight, which the events of the succeeding day may show to have been erroneous. Moreover, if from the obscure character of the case, or in the imperfection of our science, diagnosis is impossible, we should then so generalise our treatment that we may include what is possible of good, and exclude what is probable of harm.

Dr. JACOB BIGELOW
Nature in Disease, 1852.

Of Palliatives

When we know that a case is self-limited or incurable, we are to consider how far it is in our power to palliate or diminish sufferings which we are not competent to remove. Here is a most important field for medical practice, and one which calls for an exceedingly large portion of the time and efforts of every physician. When we consider that most diseases occupy, from necessity, a period of some days or weeks, that many of them continue for months, and some for years, and finally that a large portion of mankind die of some lingering or chronic disease, we shall see that the study of palliatives is not only called for, but really constitutes one of the most common, as well as the most useful and beneficent employments of a medical man.

Dr. JACOB BIGELOW
Nature in Disease, 1852.

"*Old Forgotten Far-off Things*"

It is curious how men and methods in surgery are so soon forgotten, and then unwittingly an old treatment is brought forward as a new thing or a new discovery. A good example is Bier's congestion treatment, which has been practised in Egypt for thousands of years. It is mentioned in the Proverbs, "The blueness of a wound cleanseth away evil."

Sir CHARLES BALLANCE
Remarks and Reminiscences
B.M.J., 1927.

Regimen Sanitatis Salernitanum

The Salerne Schoole doth by these lines impart
All health to Englands King, and doth advise
From care his head to keepe, from wrath his heart,
Drink not much wine, sup light, and soone arise.
When meat is gone, long sitting breedeth smart;
And after-noone still waking keep your eyes.
When mov'd you find your selfe to Natures Needs
Forbeare them not, for that much danger breeds.
Use three Physicians still; first Doctor Quiet,
Next Doctor Merry-man, and Doctor Dyet.

> *Advice imparted to (supposedly) Robert, Duke of
> Normandy, eldest son of William the Conqueror.*

Traditional Remedies

Digitalis is a notable example. In its early days it was a true old wives' cure for dropsy. Withering, in 1776, having learned from an old Shropshire woman of the virtues of the foxglove, tried it in his practice, and was convinced of its value. But he no more knew how it cured than he knew that dropsy was not a disease but a symptom of many diseases. Half a century passed before Bright drew attention to the association of renal disease with albuminous urine, and so paved the way for a distinction between renal and cardiac dropsy. And we can afford to smile at Withering's disappointment at the failure of his foxglove leaves to cure a case of ovarian cyst—then regarded as a form of dropsy. The final demonstration of the specific effect of digitalin and certain allied alkaloids upon the disorder of cardiac rhythm which we now know as auricular fibrillation belongs to the present century.

Dr. MAURICE SHAW
Medical Facts and Fallacies
B.M.J., 1936.

The falsest and most absurd notions are entertained respecting the whole subject of the morbid conditions of the animal economy, and respecting the means deemed capable of modifying and removing them.

If this ignorance of a science and art, of which there exist established professors and practitioners, were strictly confined in its effects to the individual minds lodging it, and were, like our ignorance in regard to many of the other practical arts of life, simply passive, there might be a question whether it were of much or of any importance that it should be removed. What greater necessity, it may be said, is there for men in general being enlightened in the science and art of the physician, than in the science and art of the shoemaker or tailor, of the coachbuilder, saddler, or of any of the other handicrafts subservient to his comfort and happiness?

The distinction between these arts and the medical art, in their relations with the public, is this—that whereas, in the case of the former, we are contented to let the artists take their own way without any interference on our part, in the latter (Medicine) we are perpetually interfering, actually or virtually, directly or indirectly; so that it becomes a matter of vital importance that the interference, if it does take place, should be guided by knowledge not by ignorance; or, what would be the preferable result of knowledge, that the interference should be altogether foregone.

The injurious interference here chiefly referred to as the result of ignorance of the nature of diseases and of the medical art, is not an active and direct interference with the proceedings of the physician, under the pretence of knowledge of what is for the patient's good; as such interference is only had recourse to in rare instances and by very unreasonable persons, and would only be tolerated by those who are unworthy of the medical office. What is here complained of and deprecated is the indirect influence often exercised over the conduct and practice of the physician, through the anxieties, wishes, hopes, fears, or other natural emotions of the patient or his friends, which a truer knowledge would often enable them to suppress or keep within more legitimate bounds. It is often impossible for the most scientific and honest physician to resist the influence of such causes, though he may know that some of his proceedings, the result of this influence, are hardly such as can be justified either by considerations of science or by the more rigid rules of professional propriety.

Sir JOHN FORBES
Nature and Art in Disease, 1857.

Lay Pressure

There is hardly a man living, be his disease what it may, who will bear to believe himself beyond the possibility of restoration to health. He will allow the physician to profess palliation, and postponement, and relief; and, when the physician does all which he professed to do, he will be thankful to him, but he will think it strange that he can do no more. And so he lets go his faith and his allegiance, and goes in search of some one to cure him by a lucky remedy.

Thus the comparison of what we *can* do with what we are expected to do, is often mortifying enough. But it cannot be helped. People are free to expect what they like; while we cannot do more than can be done. Our ability is bounded by the nature of things, at all events.

Dr. PETER MERE LATHAM
Lectures on Clinical Medicine, 1836.

Experiments on Patients

In incurable affections, in affections which, though often curable, are grave, only yielding slowly and after leading the patient through the greatest perils, therapeutic attempts are allowable, if they are corollaries from facts acquired under analogous circumstances, or from the successful experiments of others. When a patient runs an imminent and certain risk, it is justifiable, or at least it is excusable, to use every remedy, as in such a case we cannot make bad worse. Still, even in such cases, our therapeutic action must be defensible in theory and by an appeal to analogy. . . .

So long as the man of art only makes experiments of this kind, he will forthwith be absolved by his own conscience (and that is the most important matter), and he will likewise be acquitted by his peers, who sit on judgment on his conduct; while on the other hand he will be condemned, and justly branded, if the experiment has been performed merely to gratify curiosity. But how much more blameworthy is the man who experiments in such a fashion in a hospital, where there is not that feeling of responsibility which often makes the private practitioner tremble; where there is no necessity to guard against a compromising of position; where patients are under absolute authority, and may for disobedience be dismissed from hospital, and turned adrift without asylum or succour.

TROUSSEAU
Lectures on Clinical Medicine.

How to Use Drugs

It is my own practice to avoid drugs as much as possible;
and I more frequently find it difficult to persuade people
from using them, than to induce them to take them. But I
hope that you will not believe me to be distrustful of the
power of drugs to do real service to the sick, under proper
circumstances. I am far otherwise. And in reference to this
point, I wish to tell you that your success in the use of medicines may depend somewhat on the temper with which you
give them. You must be hopeful and feel an interest in
them. Do not, like a cold stepfather, leave them to make
their own way in the world; but watch them in their course.

JAMES JACKSON, M.D.
Letters to a young Physician, 1855.

Of Therapeutics

Of therapeutics we may say what has been said of the
legislative powers of a State. We cannot assign definite
and immutable limits to them or lay down inflexible rules
for their use. The treatment of every case of sickness must
be determined ultimately for and by itself, tentatively by
skilled men and as their practical sagacity may determine,
while they bear in mind that the virtues of a medicine depend
less upon its intrinsic properties and powers than on the
sagacity of the physician who administers it, just as the
efficiency of firearms depends less upon the explosives and
the missile they contain than on the judgment and accuracy
of aim of the man who discharges them.

Dr. ALFRED STILLÉ

Of Drugs and Placebos

I believe that we not only feed the public demand for use-less and harmful drugs, but also go far to create that very demand. Babes are not born with a desire to take a drug for every symptom—they acquire this desire. Who teaches them? You and I do. We educate our patients and their friends to believe that every or almost every symptom and disease can be benefited by a drug. Some ignorant practitioners believe this, and we cannot blame them, though we deplore the results of their indiscriminate drugging. But in my experience the educated physician who knows that only a few of his patients can be much benefited by drugs, gives out just as many prescriptions as the ignorant physician who believes all that the Pharmacopeia and the nostrum vendor tell him. The only difference is that the educated physician gives his drugs as placebos. In my opinion, the placebo habit does more harm than the habit of giving drugs to every patient with full faith in their pharmacologic action. ... They weaken the confidence of the patient in the physician because every placebo is a lie, and in the long run the lie is found out. We give a placebo with one meaning; the patient receives it with quite another. We mean him to suppose that the drug acts directly on his body, not through his mind by means of expectant attention. If the patient finds out what we are doing, he laughs at it, or is rightly angry with us. I have seen both the laughter and the anger —at our expense. Placebo giving is quackery. It also fosters the nostrum evil.

R. C. CABOT
The Physician's Responsibility for the Nostrum Evil
J.A.M.A., 1906.

Therapeutic Armarium

Long has he been of that amphibious fry,
Bold to prescribe and busie to apply,
His shop the gazing vulgar's eyes employs
With foreign trinkets and domestick toys.
Here mummies lay most reverently stale,
And there the tortoise hung her coat of mail.
Not far from some large shark's devouring head
The flying fish their finny pinions spread.
Aloft in rows large poppy heads were strung,
And near a scaly alligator hung.
In this place drugs in musty heaps decayed,
In that dried bladders and drawn teeth were laid.

Sir SAMUEL GARTH
The Dispensary, 1699.

Convalescence

The management of convalescence is worthy of a treatise in itself. As far as the friends, family or doctor are concerned, the illness has passed; the patient, though perhaps weak, is physically sound, and thus is heartily congratulated on his satisfactory and miraculous recovery, and dismissed by all hands with rejoicing. The poor patient, on the other hand, now acutely aware of very disagreeable sensations, weary and exhausted in mind or body, unconsciously exaggerates these sensations, misinterprets his symptoms, undergoes agonies of fear lest he should not recover, or imagines he is left with some incurable result, or that his illness is about to recur. Too tired to comprehend the logical reasoning of his friends and doctor, he drags on a miserable existence; until suddenly to his utter astonishment he does recover.

WARFIELD T. LONGCOPE
Methods and Medicine
Bull. Johns Hopkins Hospital, 1932.

Bishop Copplestone and His Tar Water

I did not think Copplestone, with all his nonsense, could have got down to tar-water. I have as much belief in it as I have in holy water—it is the water has done the business, not the tar. They could not induce the sensual prelate to drink water but by mixing it up with nonsense and disguising the simplicity of the receipt. You must have a pitch-battle with him about his tar-water, and teach him what he has never learnt—the rudiments of common sense.

SYDNEY SMITH
Letter to his son-in-law, Dr. Holland, 1835.

Old Time Therapeutics

For a perfect sight of the old medicine, let me conduct you to the bedside of Charles II: With a cry he fell. Dr. King, who, fortunately, happened to be present, bled him with a pocket knife. Fourteen physicians were quickly in attendance. They bled him more thoroughly; they scarified and cupped him; they shaved and blistered his head; they gave him an emetic, a clyster, and two pills. During the next eight days they "threw in" fifty-seven separate drugs; and towards the end, a cordial containing forty more. This availing nothing, they tried Goa stone, which was a calculus obtained from a species of Indian goat; and as a final remedy, the distillate of human skull. In the case report it is recorded that the emetic and the purge worked so mightily well that it was a wonder the patient died. One physician did protest that they would kill the king; and out of this arose the suspicion that he had been irregularly poisoned. But he did die, "as peaceable as a lamb"; his last words were "Do not let poor Nellie starve."

Sir ANDREW MACPHAIL
The Source of Modern Medicine
B.M.J., 1933.

Of Dealing With Children

In meeting most of the mental and spiritual problems of childhood, the force of example is the strongest weapon. Physicians must not lie to their small patients, or allow others to do so. If we must hurt them, tell them so. If you tell him that he is not going to be hurt, and then do so, you have lost his confidence, and given him a lesson in untruthfulness which he will try out for himself.

W. P. LUCAS
The Modern Practice of Pediatrics, 1927.

A Child's Terror

The hospital allowed Oliver to come home. . . . When he turned to Julia, he said: "I was afraid all the time of what they would do to me next, but I got out before they could do the worst thing of all. . . . I kept hearing them say I would have to have my bowels opened." "Oh, the terrors children suffer needlessly," Julia cried. "It only means Syrup of Figs or something of that kind." "I wish I had known," said Oliver simply.

ELIZABETH TAYLOR
At Mrs. Lippincote's, 1945.

How to Deal with Children

No one can be successful in the management of little children who has not acquired the art of hiding from them their power to disturb.

HECTOR C. CAMERON
Lancet, 1928.

The Child's Confidence

The early months of hygienic care are also establishing the infant's confidence in the whole system around him, and big things are being accomplished. The infant learns that the nurse means what she does for him, and that crying will not alter the plan as long as his condition is normal. As the child grows older that confidence must be preserved, and woe unto the physician who breaks it down. If the child must be hurt in an examination, he should not be told that it will not hurt him. He should not be lied to, or frightened.

W. P. Lucas
The Modern Practice of Pediatrics, 1927.

Young Barbarians

That unique and interesting Californian, Luther Burbank, made a most valuable suggestion in *The Training of the Human Plant*, and his words are a sound background for a technical discussion of the mind problems of a growing child. He said, "Every child should have mudpies, grasshoppers, water bugs, tadpoles, frogs, mud turtles, elderberries, wild strawberries, acorns, chestnuts, trees to climb, brooks to wade in, water lilies, woodchicks, bats, bees, butterflies, various animals to pet, hayfields, pine cones, rocks to roll, sand snakes, huckleberries and hornets, and any child who has been deprived of these has been deprived of the best part of his education." Not a calory or a vitamin, an ounce or a pound, an internal gland or an amino-acid in the list, yet perhaps that paragraph is as deeply scientific as any Burbank ever made.

W. P. Lucas
The Modern Practice of Pediatrics, 1927.

The Child's World

All the numerous and shocking mistakes that have been made—that are still being made—in the upbringing and instruction of children arise from the common conviction that a child is a miniature adult, that is, a reasonable being, capable of conviction by intellectual means. Children are creative (and destructive) by natural impulse, not through any form of reasoning. So it is by a kind of creative instinct that they like poetry. They are still living in that mysterious world to which music belongs. In their world the writs of reason do not run. Children, like the lunatic, the lover and the poet, are of imagination all compact. One sees more devils than vast hell can hold; that is, in plain prose, children populate their world with demons, fairies, witches and monsters, with talking animals and vocal trees. The lover, all as frantic, sees Helen's beauty in a brow of Egypt. Behold, then, the small girl turning with polite indifference from the finest Lenci doll to cherish her beloved Golliwog or Teddy, which lives and moves and has its being at her word, which comforts her in sorrow, and soothes her at last to sleep. Such tricks hath strong imagination. At length the man perceives it die away and fade into the light of common day.

GEORGE SAMPSON
Seven Essays.

Naughty Children

Oh, you little wretch! Your letter cost me fourpence. I will pull all the plums out of your puddings; I will undress your dolls and steal their under-petticoats; you shall have no currant-jelly to your rice; I will kiss you till you cannot see out of your eyes; when nobody else whips you, I will do so; I will fill you so full of sugar-plums that they shall run out of your nose and ears; lastly your frocks shall be so short that they shall not come below your knees.

Your loving grandfather.

SYDNEY SMITH, *to his grandchild who had sent him a letter overweight.*

V

"THIS INSUBSTANTIAL PAGEANT"

The Invalid

In this falling aside, in this quietude and desertion of other men, there is no inharmonious prelude to the last quietude and desertion of the grave; in this dulness of the senses there is a gentle preparation for the final insensibility of death. And to him the idea of mortality comes in a shape less violent and harsh than is its wont, less as an abrupt catastrophe, than as a thing in infinitesimal gradation, and the last step on a long decline of way. As we turn to and fro in bed, and every moment the movements grow feebler and smaller and the attitude more restful and easy, until sleep overtakes us at a stride, and we move no more, so desire after desire leaves him; day by day his strength decreases, and the circle of his activity grows ever narrower; and he feels, if he is to be thus tenderly weaned from the passion of life, thus gradually inducted into the slumber of death, that when at last the end comes, it will come quietly and fitly. If anything is to reconcile poor spirits to the coming of the last enemy, surely it should be such a mild approach as this; not to hale us forth with violence, but to persuade us from a place we have no further pleasure in. It is not so much, indeed, death that approaches as life that withdraws and withers up from round about him. He has outlived his own usefulness, and almost his own enjoyment; and if there is to be no recovery; if never again will he be young and strong and passionate, if the actual present shall be to him like a thing read in a book or remembered out of the far-away past; if, in fact, this be veritably nightfall, he will not wish greatly for the continuance of a twilight that only strains and disappoints the eyes, but steadfastly await the perfect darkness. He will pray for Medea; when she comes, let her either rejuvenate or slay.

ROBERT LOUIS STEVENSON
Ordered South.

Distempered Minds

The eighteenth century laughed at lunatics. Indeed, William Cowper, when a Westminster schoolboy seeing the sights of London, had visited the Hospital of St. Mary of Bethlehem, commonly called Bedlam. "I was not altogether insensible of the misery of these poor creatures," he wrote, "but the madness of them had such a humourous air, and displayed itself in so many whimsical freaks, that it was impossible not to be entertained." For a small fee sightseers could spend a long time laughing at the Bedlam lunatics; and discharged patients, no longer dangerous but still amusingly mad, could be seen in the London streets with a badge on their left arm showing they were licensed to beg. When it was Cowper's turn to be the cause of mirth he was lucky to be sent to a private asylum at St. Albans, under the care of Dr. Nathaniel Cotton, who had been trained by a famous professor of physic at Leyden.

BERNARD MARTIN, *John Newton, a Biography*, 1950.

An Eighteenth-Century Sick Room

Before John's seventh birthday, his mother was stricken with consumption. She was obliged to leave her son in London under the charge of casual neighbours, while she went to an old school-friend who had married a man named George Catlett in Chatham. Mrs. Catlett gave the sick woman the best possible attention. She was put to bed in a hot dark room, with all windows and cracks sealed. Even the key-hole in the door was stuffed up, in obedience to the current advice;

> When the air comes through a hole
> Take care of your soul.

She was made to drink snail broth and purgatives; but notwithstanding these approved methods of combating the prevalent disease, the soul of Mrs. Newton escaped, and the boy John "lost a valuable parent."

BERNARD MARTIN, *John Newton, a Biography*, 1950.

[152]

Frail House

There comes a period in most illnesses, I think, sometimes during a temporary respite, more often perhaps at the first dawn of convalescence when one becomes extraordinarily conscious, yet without discomfort, of the almost trivial delicacy of one's surrounding tissue. It is generally, I suppose, a moment of exhaustion, both mental and physical, either upon the bugle of a victory or a truce. But it is a moment when one's spiritual aesthesis, as it were, is peculiarly at liberty. Very soon, in a minute or two even, Nature will begin her work of restoration—none more willing than she, given a very little patience and half a straw to make her bricks with. But now she is standing by for a moment, trowel in hand, and the outer wind is breathing through the gap. And it's then, I think, if you'll only listen carefully enough, that you can sometimes hear it whispering.

"Presently," you can hear it say, "this little house of yours will be mended, and the more easily maybe, because its walls are so thin. But don't—don't forget too quickly that it is but a house after all."

Yet I suppose we do forget it, most of us, and probably quite healthily when once the dwelling-place is bricked up again, and the new paint is on, and it stands foursquare to the winds that may not enter now. And yet again, if the message has once been heard, or twice, or thrice, as circumstances have it, I don't believe that it is ever entirely lost. And there, perhaps, may even lie the key to all the mystery; so that when the last storm blows, and Nature must shake her head, and let the frail house fall, its tenant may not go out altogether unprepared.

PETER HARDING, M.D.
The Corner of Harley Street.

Sensible Advice

Then shall the Minister examine whether the sick person repent him truly of his sins, and be in charity with all the world; exhorting him to forgive, from the bottom of his heart, all persons that have offended him; and if he hath offended any other, to ask them forgiveness; and where he hath done injury or wrong to any man, that he makes amends to the uttermost of his power. And if he hath not before disposed of his goods, let him then be admonished to make his Will, and to declare his Debts, what he oweth and what is owing unto him; for the better discharging of his conscience, and the quietness of his Executors. But men should often be put in remembrance to take order for the settling of their temporal estates, whilst they are in health.

From the Anglican Office of the Visitation of the Sick.

" The Lord of Life and Death "

Dearly beloved, know this, that Almighty God is the Lord of life and death, and of all things to them pertaining, as youth, strength, health, age, weakness, sickness. Wherefore, whatsoever your sickness is, know you certainly that it is God's visitation. And for what cause soever this sickness is sent unto you; whether it be to try your patience for the example of others, and that your faith may be found in the day of the Lord laudable, glorious and honourable, to the increase of glory and endless felicity; or else it be sent to you to correct and amend in you whatsoever doth offend the eyes of your heavenly Father; know you certainly that if you truly repent of your sins, and bear your sickness patiently, trusting in God's mercy, for His dear Son Jesus Christ's sake, and render unto Him humble thanks for His fatherly visitation, submitting yourself wholly unto His will, it shall turn to your profit, and help you forward in the right way that leadeth unto everlasting life.

From the Anglican Office of the Visitation of the Sick.

In a Time of Pestilence

Adieu! farewell earth's bliss!
This world uncertain is:
Fond are life's lustful joys,
Death proves them all but toys.
None from his darts can fly:
I am sick, I must die—
  Lord, have mercy on us!

Rich men, trust not in wealth,
Gold cannot buy you health;
Physic himself must fade;
All things to end are made;
The plague full swift goes by;
I am sick, I must die—
  Lord, have mercy on us!

Beauty is but a flower
Which wrinkles will devour:
Brightness falls from the air;
Queens have died young and fair;
Dust hath closed Helen's eye;
I am sick, I must die—
  Lord, have mercy on us!

Strength stoops unto the grave,
Worms feed on Hector brave;
Swords may not fight with fate;
Earth still holds ope her gate;
Come! come! the bells do cry;
I am sick, I must die—
  Lord, have mercy on us!

Wit with his wantonness
Tasteth death's bitterness;
Hell's executioner
Hath no ears for to hear
What vain art can reply;
I am sick, I must die—
    Lord, have mercy on us!

Haste, therefore, each degree
To welcome destiny;
Heaven is our heritage;
Earth but a player's stage.
Mount we unto the sky;
I am sick, I must die—
    Lord, have mercy on us!

THOMAS NASHE, 1593.

Disgraceful Illnesses

"And to require the help of medicine, not when a wound
has to be cured, or on occasion of an epidemic, but just
because, by indolence and a habit of life such as we have
been describing, men fill themselves with waters and winds,
as if their bodies were a marsh, compelling the ingenious sons
of Asclepius to find more names for diseases, such as flatulence
and catarrh; is not this, too, a disgrace?"

"Yes," he said, "they do certainly give very strange and
new-fangled names to diseases."

"Yes," I said, "and I do not believe there were any such
diseases in the days of Asclepius."

PLATO
Republic.

[156]

Horace Walpole's Gout

Madame de Bouxois, Marshal Berwick's daughter, assured me that there was nothing so good for the gout as to preserve the parings of my nails in a bottle close-stoppered.

HORACE WALPOLE, *in a letter to Thomas Gray.*

An Unusual Mishap

The patient was a middle-aged man, rather thin and pale. He said that for a number of years he had suffered at times from pain in the region of the stomach after food. Recently vomiting had troubled him. This took place at irregular intervals, the amount being copious. On going into details he remembered bringing up material that he had eaten many hours before. The vomit was offensive as a rule. He was prone to violent and foul-smelling eructations. But what really distressed him more than anything else was the following startling occurrence.

One evening he had taken his wife to the cinema. There, in the darkness, feeling inclined to smoke, he had taken out a cigarette, and put it between his lips; he struck a match, bringing it up in his cupped fingers. Just at that moment a violent eructation occurred. To his alarm and astonishment, and of those seated near him, there was a flash and a sharp explosion; the cigarette was blown from his lips away across several rows of seats; his moustache was singed, and his lips and fingers burnt. In pain and confusion he had hurriedly to leave the cinema. The astonishment of the neighbours at this "fiery exhalation" can well be imagined.

. . . At laparotomy a cicatrised ulcer was found at the pylorus.

Dr. TERENCE EAST
Lancet, 1934.

An Obedient Patient

Mary Clarke was launched on her career by Madame Récamier. About 1830, her mother, who suffered from bronchitis, was forbidden ever to go into the fresh air again; the whole of Mrs. Clarke's life must be spent indoors, and Madame Récamier who admired her character and attainments invited her to come and live in her house, the Abbaye-aux-Bois. Mrs. Clarke obeyed these instructions, and lived to be ninety-two.

CECIL WOODHAM-SMITH
Florence Nightingale.

Brave to Endure

I do not regard it as heroic to die when there is no time to be conscious either of fear or pain. Let us keep the word "heroic" for those who consciously endure anguish, for those to whom fear and pain are ever present. Those men and women who lie in bed and see the day dawn through the blind, and hear the life of the streets begin again, the sound of some cart moving, the sound of some belated motor changing gear—those men and women who thus lying know the dawn means for them another day of pain, another day of fearing the great cycles of pain which wheel inexorably around their bed—those men and women who, knowing this and dreading this, can still keep courage, can still face the grim tyrannies of pain and fear with a derisive smile: those people are my heroes. The people who have time to fear and time to suffer: the people to whom every sunset is red with agony and every dawn is chill with fear. Let us, when faced with sudden tragedy in its most appalling form, remember that no sudden tragedy can be so terrible as one that is prolonged, no courage can be so magnificent as that which knows, which waits, but which can still endure.

HAROLD NICOLSON

Malade Malgré Lui

It's the penalty, I suppose, of being rarely laid aside by sickness, that when some trivial misfortune does make its appearance one exaggerates its proportion in the general scheme of things to a quite unmerited degree—and especially, I think, if one happens to be a doctor. "Physician, heal thyself," the mockers say. But he should never attempt to. He knows too much about the various possibilities, the remoter significances of each one of his little troubles, to be a sufficiently clear-minded judge. And he is far better advised when he resigns his body *in toto* to the care of some outside mind, and confines his own mental powers to the fortification of his private philosophy.

PETER HARDING, M.D.
The Corner of Harley Street.

Sickness

Put all the miseries that man is subject to together, *sicknesse* is more than all. It is the *immediate* sword of God. *Phalaris* could invent a Bull; and others have invented Wheels and Racks; but no persecutor could ever invent a *sicknesse* or a way to inflict a *sicknesse* upon a condemned man: To a *galley* he can send him, and to the *gallows*, and command execution that hour; but to a *quartane fever*, or to a *gout*, he cannot condemn him. In *poverty* I lack but other things; In *banishment* I lack other men; but in *sicknesse*, I lack my *self*. And, as the greatest misery of war is when our own Country is made the seat of the war; so is it of *affliction*, when *mine own Body* is made the subject thereof. How shall I put a just value upon God's great *blessings* of *Wine*, and *Oyle*, and *Milke*, and *Honey*, when my taste is gone, or of *Liberty*, when the *gout* fetters my feet?

JOHN DONNE
Sermon XX.

A Child's Illness

As soon as we took up our new quarters I became severely ill and nearly died. I mention this fact because it had an important effect on my development. I learned afterwards, from my mother's talk to visitors, that my recovery was regarded as a kind of miracle—the tale lost nothing in the telling. Of that illness I have not the slightest recollection, I know of it only from my mother's oft-told tale. Here, indeed, a psychologist would rightly put his finger on a bad spot in my growth. I had been almost fatally ill, with no knowledge of the fact; but I was never allowed to forget it. I was always the little boy who nearly died, and recovered miraculously. I was very delicate, was always described as delicate, and so grew up with that kind of taint upon me. Suddenly the curtain lifts for a moment, and I am clearly aware of a child in a large bed with one of those old-fashioned patchwork quilts beloved of the young. I see my mother with a strange, bearded, spectacled man called the doctor, and on the bed is a Noah's Ark with its animals scattered about, and a book, my very first book, a large and highly coloured Alphabet Book, beginning "A was an Archer who shot at a Frog." Obviously I am getting well, or there would be no such book. I see also a dish containing eggs, each with something scribbled on it. I ask the doctor what the scribble means, and he tells me that it is the date when the eggs were laid, so that we can be sure they are fresh. I am astonished, and ask how chickens can know the date. I am told that I must not ask questions, but lie still and get well. I assure him that it does not hurt me to ask questions; but the mystery of the date is not explained. Then the curtain falls; and when it rises I am a little boy of five in knickerbockers. Illness and alphabet book are totally forgotten, for I am alive and well and running about, and greatest mystery of all, I can read.

GEORGE SAMPSON, *Seven Essays.*

On the Gout

I have gout, asthma, and seven other maladies but am otherwise very well. . . . Gout is the only enemy that I do not wish to have at my feet. . . . What an admirable provision of Providence is the gout! What prevents human beings from making the body a larder or a cellar but the gout? When I feel a pang, I say, "I know what this is for. I know what you mean. I understand the hint!" and so I endeavour to extract a little wisdom from pain.

SYDNEY SMITH
Letter to Mrs. Meynell, 1840.

Clinical Picture

Morton quotes an early clinician, who describes a man suffering from belladonna poisoning as being "hot as a hare, blind as a bat, dry as a bone, red as a beet, and mad as a hen." This seems to put the matter in a nutshell.

PERIPATETIC
In England Now
Lancet.

The Name of Syphilis

Hieronymus Fracastorius, born at Verona in 1482 (ten years before Columbus discovered America) wrote about the three scourges which followed in the track of the armies which ravaged Italy. His Latin poem on the new venereal disease described how the local sun-god had punished the world because the swineherd Syphilis ("pig-lover") had sacrificed not to him but to the local King. The learned who read the poem found the name appropriate for the beastly disease.

Lancet, *annotation.*

Sydney Smith's Hay Fever

I am suffering from my old complaint, the hay-fever (as it is called). My fear is of perishing by deliquescence—I melt away in nasal and lachrymal profluvia. My remedies are warm pediluvium, cathartics, topical application of a watery solution of opium to eyes, ears and the interior of the nostrils. The membrane is so irritable that light, dust, contradiction, an absurd remark, the sight of a dissenter—anything, sets me a-sneezing, and if I begin sneezing at twelve, I don't leave off till two o'clock—and am heard distinctly in Tarenton when the wind sets that way, at a distance of six miles. Turn your mind to this little curse. If consumption is too powerful for physicians, at least they should not suffer themselves to be outwitted by such little upstart disorders as the hay-fever.

Letter to his son-in-law, Dr. Holland, 1835.

How it Looks to the Patient

It is curious. Your sensations during fever are nearly indistinguishable from pleasant ones, and yet there is a mockery about them all. To have a high temperature is the most splendid (and most unfair) sermon on the vanity of physical pleasures. You are consumed with the most promising thirst; there at your elbow stands the long, cool drink. You drink. What an uncanny and distressing disproportion appears between the glorious magnitude of that craving and the tiny satisfaction it brings! This tired, tender ache which is all over you like a voluptuous feeling, seems to promise deepest rest; but the exquisite diminuendo of consciousness does not ensue! This fine sensitiveness to the chill of sheets hints that it will be delightful to nestle into warmth. The glow comes. Good heavens! it was not warmth you wanted! Turn the pillow, try the other side—there's a little cool strip left for one leg, at any rate, between the hang-over and the mattress.

Everyone has experienced these feverish sensations. The peculiarity about them which makes them distressful, is not so much that they are unpleasant in themselves as acutely tantalising; they are cravings associated with deep satisfactions which never follow. One's whole sensuous being is continually concentrated in expectation, and continually cheated.

Sir DESMOND MACCARTHY
The New Statesman, 1927.

Convalescence

The great thing is that he is getting better. Emerging from the gloom and peril of his illness into the cheerful light of day, he finds that all the surroundings so familiar in his ordinary life have somehow acquired during his absence a new interest and delight. He bethinks himself that he might never have seen them again, and he looks upon them with a sense at once of their preciousness and their precariousness. He reflects that after all it is only a reprieve that has been granted to him, and his renewed appreciation of the world around him is in a way enhanced by his realisation of its inevitable transitoriness.

There is one blessed dispensation for which the convalescent cannot be too grateful, and that is the speediness with which the memory of pain passes into oblivion. We are so constituted that we cannot recall the actual sensations of past suffering. We know that we have experienced long days and weeks of acute misery, but they seem to recede from our consciousness like a nightmare dispelled by the return of daylight. "Forgetfulness" is here indeed "life's best balm."

LORD MACMILLAN
Sunday Times, 1950.

The Genial Sense of Youth

In a hospital distinguished for its highly scientific methods, special studies were being made of renal function, for which a number of aged nephritics in the wards provided the necessary material. A fourth-year student, who happened to be a reformed osteopath, was at the time acting as a clinical clerk. Observing that there was no special treatment prescribed for these cases, he asked if he might see what he could do. He might, of course. So that evening, after the ward was smoothly tucked in for the night, he went to the bedside of a man in whom the disease was advanced and said, "John, what do you really complain of anyway?" "Backache, and I can't sleep," said John. "That's easily fixed," said the student. "Your spine's out of joint. Turn over on your face." So the immaculate coverlets were disarranged while John's back was given some deep massage. The next morning, after an unusually comfortable night, he told the somewhat annoyed head nurse that at last he had found a doctor who could do something for him.

HARVEY CUSHING
Consecratio Medici, 1929.

As Little Children

Old persons are sometimes as unwilling to die as tired-out children are to say good night and go to bed.

J. S. LE FANU

Death and the Aged

O Death, acceptable is thy sentence unto the needy and unto him whose strength faileth, that is now in the last age, and is vexed with all things, and to him that despaireth and hath lost patience.   *Ecclesiasticus.*

Old Age

The seas are quiet when the winds give o'er;
So calm are we when passions are no more.
For then we know how vain it is to boast
Of fleeting things, so certain to be lost.
Clouds of affection from our younger eyes
Conceal that emptiness which age descries.

The soul's dark cottage, batter'd and decay'd,
Lets in new light through chinks that time hath made:
Stronger by weakness, wiser men become
As they draw near to their eternal home.
Leaving the old, both worlds at once they view
That stand upon the threshold of the new.

EDMUND WALLER, 1606-1687.

" Good and Faithful "

Apart from teaching, my job in life has centred round the examination of the body after death and the lesson which I am continually learning from post-mortem examinations is the versatility and courage, the ingenuity and determination with which the body strives to keep our house from tumbling about our ears. I do not wonder that people die; that is easy enough. What I marvel at is that they go on living with bodies so maimed, disordered, and worn out. In the end, when it has done all it can, the body has to give in and we have to fall out of this splendid procession of life; but it is not from idleness or wilfulness, and as I come away from the post-mortem room I often feel inclined to say "Well done, good and faithful."

Grains and Scruples
Lancet.

Ripe and Mellow

Just as apples, when unripe, are torn from trees, but, when ripe and mellow, drop down, so it is violence that takes life from young men, ripeness from old. This ripeness is so delightful to me, that, as I approach nearer to death, I seem, as it were, to be sighting land, and to be coming to port at last after a long voyage.

CICERO
De Senectute.

Of Old Age

I go back to some of those curious experiences which happen to the aged. *Morituri te salutamus,* as every old man must whisper as he greets the circle of his acquaintance and waves to them his farewell. One sensation, very difficult to describe, seems appropriate, as though Nature with kindly intent was trying to make things relatively pleasant to her worn-out children. It comes sometimes in the morning when one is beginning another day, sometimes on going to bed when one realises that another date has to be wiped off the calendar. The odd feeling prevails of a "distance," ever growing, and life moving steadily to some close. A steady disappearance is the prevalent idea. Life has come and poured its treasures in our laps and now is asking for each several treasure to be returned. It was only a loan, not a gift; it never belonged to us, and now can be recalled—whatever may be the particular treasure which we have cherished and called our own. To one man this perhaps might be physical strength, which distinguished him above his fellows: or it might be a personality of singular charm: or it might be an acute brain, or clearly logical intellect. Or, again, it might be the boon of art, music, or poetry, or dramatic skill. These things belonged to us once, and now are slowly withdrawn. They are ours no more. . . .

But of all the unhappy aspects that old age can show to men and women looking with a certain dread to an uncertain future, the worst, I think, is boredom. Boredom in one shape or another is inevitable. As you change from one phase of life to another, as your youth lapses into middle age, and manhood—or the complete functioning of all your powers—into old age, the thought recurs now and again to your mind, when all the various interests that occupy your life have disappeared and sunk into nothingness, what shall you be able to substitute for these eager passions and desires? How shall you fill the void? And then comes the slow and painful discovery that the void cannot be filled, and that yours must be a truncated life—beginning, in other words, the slow descent into an Avernus of dulness and apathy. Others have been through this stage before you, and you can gather whatever consolation is possible from that fact. But it does not give you a lasting felicity: it leaves you confronted as before, with a blank wall of indifference and passivity. For the worst of the situation is that you have become careless even of those subjects which used to give you such keen delight. It is a sore disappointment to find Plato tasteless and Virgil wearisome—only Koheleth affords a temporary distraction, in that splendid last chapter of Ecclesiastes in which he records his experience that "All is vanity."

W. L. Courtney
Moriturus
The Nation, 1927.

The Summons

One evil in old age is that as your time is come, you think every little illness is the beginning of the end. When a man expects to be arrested, every knock at the door is an alarm.

Sydney Smith

Second Childhood

Strange as it may seem, the majority of senile patients cling to life and fear death, although this fear commonly disappears shortly before death itself, when it is regarded as a welcome release. . . .

Therefore the will to live and the hope of recovery must be encouraged and the loss of self-restraint and self-respect met by a cheerful optimism on the part of the doctor in which mild jokes, cheerful chaff, and the avoidance of sympathetic condolence all play their parts. Remember we are dealing with second childhood when the old adage "little things please little minds" has again become true, and if the aged are easily upset, they are, like children, easily reassured and comforted by those in whom they have placed their confidence. But you can only jest in this fashion with elderly patients when you know them. Again, like children, they often resent what seems to them familiarity at an early stage of acquaintance.

Dr. DOUGLAS FIRTH
Lancet, 1934.

Past Seventy

It is a bore, I admit, to be past seventy, for you are left for execution and are daily expecting the death-warrant; but it is not anything very capital we quit. We are, at the close of life, only hurried away from stomach-aches, pains in the joints, from sleepless nights and unamusing days, from weakness, ugliness and nervous tremors; but we shall all meet again in another planet, cured of all our defects. Rogers will be less irritable, Macaulay more silent, Hallam will assent, Jeffrey will speak slower, Bolus will be just as he is, I shall be more respectful to the upper clergy.

SYDNEY SMITH

Beautiful Old Age

It ought to be lovely to be old
to be full of the peace that comes of experience
and wrinkled ripe fulfilment.

The wrinkled smile of completeness that follows a life
lived undaunted and unsoured with accepted lies.
If people lived without accepting lies
they would ripen like apples, and be scented like pippins
in their old age.

Soothing, old people should be, like apples
when one is tired of love.
Fragrant like yellowing leaves and dim with the soft
stillness and satisfaction of autumn.

And a girl should say:
It must be wonderful to live and to grow old.
Look at my mother, how rich and still she is!

And a young man should think: By Jove
my father has faced all weathers, but it's been a life!

D. H. LAWRENCE
Pansies.

Death and an Old Man

An *Old Man* that had travell'd a great way under a huge
burden of sticks, found himself so weary, that he cast it
down, and call'd upon *Death* to deliver him from a more
miserable life. *Death* came presently at his call, and asked
him his business. Pray, good sir, says he, do me but the
favour to help me up with my burden again.

AESOP
Fables
Translated by Sir Roger L'Estrange.

The Rights of the Old

I remember, many years ago, a woman in the seventies who was highly indignant with her own medical man because he had told her that she was too old for an operation. Her words of reproach, to the effect that "old people had as much right to be relieved as young ones" have always been a guiding principle with me, and I have often proved their justification.

Professor GREY TURNER
B.M.J., 1932.

Never Say Die

An old lady who was looking forward to the near approach of her hundredth birthday had the misfortune to have a fall in her house, and to bruise—but only slightly—her face on the carpet. The family sent off at once for the family doctor, who was greeted by the old lady asking "Doctor, shall I be disfigured for life?"

Current Story.

Humour Them!

The real secret of treating any old people is to let them have their own way, or to make them think that they are getting it. There is no surer way of rapidly finishing off an old patient than to impose on him a strict regime of any kind, whether dietary, medicinal or even just insisting on his bed being immaculate. In such circumstances old people rapidly come to the conclusion, consciously or otherwise, that life is no longer worth living and quickly slide away in spite of all medical and nursing care. Relax the reins as much as possible, humour them in every way legitimately possible, if it should be against accepted canons for treating a similar state in younger patients, and it is extraordinary how often they will pick up.

Dr. W. N. LEAK
Practitioner, 1948.

" We Cease Gradually "

Observe in all the ordinary changes and declinations we undergo, how nature hides from us the sight of our loss and decay. What remains to an old man of the vigour of his youth and of past days? I do not believe we should be able to endure such a change if it came upon us all at once; but nature leads us by the hand little by little down a gentle and imperceptible slope, step by step, and so lowers us to it. So that we feel no shock when youth dies in us, though this is in essence and reality a harder death than the final dissolution of a feeble body, which is nothing more than the death of old age.

MONTAIGNE

" Am I not a Brother and a Man "

We but follow each other through the furnace of affliction, as we follow each other to the grave. Who of us has so hedged in his earthly treasures that the spoiler cannot easily break through the frail enclosure, and rifle him, in a moment, of the choicest and best?

> The spider's most attenuated thread
> Is cord, is cable, to man's tender tie
> On earthly bliss—it breaks at every breeze.

We are brothers, then, in all the liabilities and contingencies and uncertainties of the future. Let us be brothers and fellow helpers, also, in its hopes and its duties.

ELISHA BARTLETT, *in a letter to Dr. Green.*

Mortality

Man with his burning soul
Has but an hour of breath
To build a ship of truth
In which his soul may sail—
Sail on the sea of death,
For death takes toll
Of beauty, courage, youth,
Of all but truth.

JOHN MASEFIELD
Philip the King, 1914.

The Sting of Mortality

Remember that the companionship of time is but of short duration. It flies more quickly than the shades of evening. We are like a child that grasps in his hand a sunbeam. He opens his hand soon again, but to his amazement finds it empty and the brightness gone.

YEDAYA PENINI
Provençal Jewish Philosopher, 1270-1340.

All Things to End are Made

. . . What if some little paine the passage have,
That makes fraile flesh to feare the bitter wave?
Is not short paine well borne, that brings long ease,
And layes the soule to sleepe in quiet grave?
Sleep after toyle, port after stormie seas,
Ease after warre, death after life does greatly please.

EDMUND SPENSER

[172]

The Shadow

Mr. Casaubon, with an unmistakable desire to end the conversation, waved his hand slightly, and said again, "I thank you," proceeding to remark on the rare beauty of the day.

Lydgate, certain that his patient wished to be alone, soon left him; and the black figure with hands behind and head bent forward continued to pace the walk where the dark yew-trees gave him a mute companionship in melancholy, and the little shadows of bird or leaf that fleeted across the isles of sunlight, stole along in silence as in the presence of a sorrow. Here was a man who now for the first time found himself looking into the eyes of death—who was passing through one of those rare moments of experience when we feel the truth of a common-place, which is as different from what we call knowing it, as the vision of waters upon the earth is different from the delirious vision of water which cannot be had to cool the burning tongue. When the common-place "We must all die" transforms itself suddenly into the acute consciousness "I must die—and soon," then death grapples us, and his fingers are cruel; afterwards, he may come to fold us in his arms as our mother did, and our last moment of dim earthly discerning may be like the first. To Mr. Casaubon, now it was as if he suddenly found himself on the dark river-brink and heard the plash of the oncoming oar, not discerning the forms, but expecting the summons.

GEORGE ELIOT
Middlemarch.

Dr. Joseph Stevens

He said in his old age: "I hope that when I go people will not say 'I'm sorry he's dead,' but 'I'm glad he lived.'"

KATHLEEN E. INNES
Hampshire Pilgrimages.

The Great Leveller

Death comes equally to us all, and makes us all equall when it comes. The ashes of an Oak in the Chimney, are no Epitaph of that Oak, to tell me how high or how large that was; It tels me not what flocks it sheltered while it stood, nor what men it hurt when it fell. The dust of great persons graves is speechlesse too, it sayes nothing, it distinguishes nothing: As soon the dust of a wretch whom thou wouldest not, as of a Prince whom thou couldest not look upon, will trouble thine eyes, if the winde blow it thither; and when a whirle-winde hath blowne the dust of the Church-yard into the Church, and the man sweeps out the dust of the Church into the Church-yard, who will undertake to sift those dusts again, and to pronounce, This is the Patrician, this is the noble flowre, and this the yeomanly, this the Plebeian bran. . . .

JOHN DONNE
Sermon XV.

Deathbeds: Sydney Smith

In looking for his medicine, the nurse found half a bottle of ink in the place where it ought to have been, and said jokingly that he had probably taken a dose of ink the previous time by mistake. "Then bring me all the blotting paper in the house," said Sydney.

HESKETH PEARSON
The Smith of Smiths.

Mr. Culpepper's End

Mr. Culpepper's death-bed expressions were remarkable; and, as they described him, in his moral inclinations, they ought not to be omitted.

His wife said to him, "Sweet heart, how canst thou be so cheerful when grim death doth look thee in the face?" He answered, "My dearest girl (his usual expression), live as I have done, and then thou wilt die as I do. For now I speak it, when it is no time to dissemble in the presence of God and His angels, I did by all persons as I would they should do by me. I was always just in my practice; I never gave my patient two medicines when one would serve the turn. Farewell, my dearest, I am spent." Shortly after these expressions he expired.

Professional Anecdotes, 1825.

Deathbeds: Rabelais

When Rabelais, who was a physician, was lying on his death-bed, and they had given him the extreme unction, a friend called and asked him how he did. Rabelais answered, "I am going my journey; they have greased my boots already."

Professional Anecdotes, 1825.

Deathbeds: Mr Belchier

Mr. Belchier, a surgeon in Sun-Court, was a stout, strong, heavy man. A few hours before he died, he fell on the floor; when his man-servant, not being able to lift him, offered to go for help, he said, "No, John, I am dying; fetch me a pillow, I may as well die here as any where else;" and shortly afterwards he expired.

Gentleman's Magazine, 1743.

William Hunter's Last Hours

A short period before he died, he rose from his bed to deliver an introductory lecture on the Operations of Surgery, in opposition to the earnest remonstrances of his friends. The lecture was accordingly delivered, but it was his last. Towards the conclusion, his strength was so much exhausted that he fainted away, and was finally replaced in his chamber, which he had been so eager to quit. Turning to his friend Combe, in his latter moments, he observed, "If I had strength enough to hold a pen, I would write how easy and pleasant a thing it is to die." His death took place on the 30th of March 1783. *Physic and Physicians*, 1842.

Deathbeds: Sir William Osler

"I have been too far across the river to go back and have it all over again."

Indulgences for Those About to Die

On Friday, June 25 (1784), I dined with Johnson at General Paoli's, where, he says in one of his letters to Mrs. Thrale, "I love to dine." There was a variety of dishes much to his taste, of all which he seemed to me to eat so much that I was afraid he might be hurt by it; and I whispered to the General my fear, and begged he might not press him. "Alas!" (said the General), "see how very ill he looks; he can live but a very short time. Would you refuse any slight gratifications to a man under sentence of death? There is a humane custom in Italy by which persons in that melancholy situation are indulged with having whatever they like best to eat and drink, even with expensive delicacies."

BOSWELL
Life of Johnson.

"Not Strive Officiously to Keep Alive"

When a cure is impossible, it is the duty of the physician to bring contentment, comfort or even happiness to his patients to lighten the burden of their affliction. But this does not mean necessarily that he should limit living to prolong life. As I grow older, I have less and less sympathy with the conscientious efforts merely to extend life in old age. The curtailment of activities, the tender nursing, the humane and assiduous attention of the doctors are apt, too frequently, to carry the aged tottering by the danger point, and leave them helpless doddering wrecks of humanity. Having arrived at this stage, it seems beyond their power, or desire, to let go the one thing they possess, that shred of life that ties them uselessly to earth. The philosophy of Stevenson's "Aes Triplex" suits me better. He says, "We do not, properly speaking, love life but living." And again, "Does not life go down with better grace, foaming in full body over a precipice, than miserably straggling to an end in sandy deltas?" It is the duty of the doctor to preserve not only health and life, but joy of living, and if most of us had to make our choice we would take the latter. Why ward off death if in the attempt we kill living? But these, perhaps, are matters over which we have but slight control. The vigorously minded patient knows the hounds are in pursuit, and keeps up the chase in spite of our earnest protest and our pleadings to seek shelter.

WARFIELD T. LONGCOPE
Methods and Medicine
Bull. Johns Hopkins Hospital, 1932.

Management of the Dying

The best medical advice, as a rule, is to the effect that the relatives have said good-bye in stages: they have seen the best of their patient. They should not try to call back a mind that is peacefully wandering, or discourage a sedative for an over-active brain. If there are words, the meaning of which it is not easy to comprehend, we should be content to leave them obscure—it may be just a dream. The phrase "death agony" is ill-chosen. In the ordinary way dying should be peaceful, or be relieved into quietude by sedatives. Best of all, there should be a good nurse. The doctor is rarely present himself. The correct attitude is to have been near at hand without intruding and to surrender his charge to the nurse in the last hours.

Dr. HUGH BARBER
Practitioner, 1948.

Triumph in Defeat

The situation demands above all humanity and common sense. Humanity, kindliness and integrity will often be required as seldom in other branches of medicine. The gleam of recognition, the look of gratitude and trust of the dying man as he becomes aware of the doctor's presence in the room may have no financial value, but it is a most satisfying reward—the culmination often of a long battle with death that patient and doctor have fought together with courage and determination; the acknowledgement that although the last enemy has won, the patient has still confidence in his physician, and the human spirit can triumph even in the hour of defeat.

Dr. W. N. LEAK
Practitioner, 1948.

Moribundus

During the last days or weeks there is obviously nothing we can do. Dully we watch life flickering, now bright, now dim. We turn to the doctor to do all he can for the sinking patient—and for us. When he can do no more, is he going to leave us to unbroken vigil with instructions to send round for the certificate when it is all over? We know he cannot cure the patient now but we do hope he will look in just to make sure there is nothing further he can do to ease the passing, and to set our minds at rest. How glad we are if he merely feels the pulse and remarks, "There's no change. Marvellous how the old heart keeps at its job. A remarkable woman, your mother." How relieved if he commands us, "You get off to bed. You're whacked. Nothing is going to happen to-night."

And when it is all over, don't we long to be reassured that everything possible has been done and nothing left undone? A very elderly farm labourer once told the writer: "I shall always remember our old doctor the time my mother died. I was only a youngster at the time, about 22. She'd been ill some weeks and I'd been doing my best to look after her. He said, 'You got nothing to reproach yourself with, bor: you've been a good son.' That made me cry a rummun. I shall never forget that."

PETER QUINCE
The Ordeal of Chronic Illness
Med. Press, 1948.

An Epitaph to Earn

When he died, the little children cried in the streets.

J. L. MOTLEY
The Rise of the Dutch Republic
(Said of William the Silent.)

Death as Friend

No human being can rest for any time in a state of equilibrium, where the desire to live, and that to depart just balance each other. If one has a house, which he has lived and always means to live in, he pleases himself with the thought of all the conveniences it offers him, and thinks little of its wants and imperfections. But once having made up his mind to move to a better, every incommodity starts out upon him, until the very ground-plan of it seems to have changed in his mind, and his thoughts and affections, each one of them packing up his little bundle of circumstances, have quitted their several chambers and nooks and migrated to the new home, long before its apartments are ready to receive their bodily tenant. It is so with the body. Most persons have died before they expire—died to all earthly longings, so that the last breath is only, as it were, the locking of the door of the already deserted mansion. The fact of the tranquillity with which the great majority of dying persons await this locking of those gates of life through which its airy angels have been going and coming, from the moment of the first cry, is familiar to those who have been often called upon to witness the last period of life. Almost always there is a preparation made by Nature for unearthing a soul, just as on a smaller scale there is for the removal of a milk-tooth. The roots which hold human life to earth are absorbed before it is lifted from its place. Some of the dying are weary and want rest, the idea of which is almost inseparable in the human mind from death. Some are in pain, and want to be rid of it, even though the anodyne be dropped, as in the legend, from the sword of the Death-Angel. Some are stupid, mercifully narcotised that they may go to sleep without long tossing about. And some are strong in faith and hope, so that, as they draw near the next world, they would fain hurry toward it, as the caravan moves faster over the sands when the foremost travellers send word along the file that water is in sight. Though each little party that follows in a foot-track of its own will have it that the water to which others think they are hastening is a mirage, not the less has it been true in all ages for human beings of every creed which recognised a future, that those who have fallen worn out by their march through the Desert have dreamed at least of a River of Life, and thought they heard its murmurs as they lay dying.

The change from the clinging to the present to the welcoming of the future comes very soon, for the most part, after all hope of life is extinguished, provided this be left in good degree to Nature, and not insolently and cruelly forced upon those who are attacked by illness, on the strength of that odious foreknowledge often imparted by science, before the white fruit whose core is ashes, and which we call *death*, has set beneath the pallid and drooping flower of sickness. There is a singular sagacity very often shown in a patient's estimate of his own vital force. His physician knows the state of his material frame well enough, perhaps—that this or that organ is more or less impaired or disintegrated; but the patient has a sense that he can hold out so much longer, —sometimes that he must and will live for a while, though by the logic of disease he ought to die without any delay.

OLIVER WENDELL HOLMES
The Professor at the Breakfast-Table.

Coming to an End

When there is no longer any hope of recovery, but plans have been made for nursing and relief of symptoms, there is an art in allowing the relatives to take charge, while the doctor recedes into a more secondary position. He must, however, have gained such confidence that there will be no catching at straws, or chasing false philosophies, which only lead to distress. We shall assume that it has been agreed that everything possible has been done. With the situation accepted that someone is in the hands of Providence or nature, it is surprising how much assistance the doctor may give; mostly in the form of reassurance. The question may be raised whether a man should be told he is going to die, although this situation may arise some little time before the expected event. Perhaps a wife has found it rather a strain to hear him talking of the future. In most cases we shall find that he has a fairly shrewd idea. He may have noticed that the more serious attempts at treatment are dropping off. He has probably picked up a hint from the doctor's words or looks. At the back of his mind he realises that, humanly speaking, his life is coming to an end; he suspects that he is just building castles in the air—and why not?—to some extent he has done it all his life. To have the admitted truth accepted by all around makes his situation uncomfortable. It is along these lines that the relatives should be advised.

Dr. Hugh Barber
Practitioner, 1948.

Bodily Dissolution

Looking down upon the dead face, touching the cold hand, lifting up the leaden arm, one cannot help feeling how utterly dead a dead man looks, an impression enormously deepened, as a rule, by the circumstances of the last days. For in these his external, his spiritual activities have been, of necessity almost, set aside, and perhaps temporarily forgotten in the paramount appeals of his body itself. Now this organ, now that, must be attended to, supported, cleansed, stimulated, implored, as it were, to fulfil its duty towards the struggling economy of the whole. And as an almost inevitable result their slender responses, their final refusals, have obsessed both patient and friends to the exclusion of everything else. The bodily case, so long taken for granted, and now so fast giving way, has become no longer a subordinate, but the predominant factor in its owner's entity. So that when the body, *Imperator et Dux* of these later hours, at length lays down its sceptre, it's a small wonder if all else has appeared to die with it.

PETER HARDING, M.D.
The Corner of Harley Street.

One Way of Survival

The small girl, during her grandfather's last illness, was sent to stay at a house where there were a number of taxidermic specimens. On her return, she made no comment on the old man's absence for some time, till one morning she remarked "I do miss grandpa; I wonder we never thought of having him stuffed."

The Countryman, 1948.

"Our Minutes Hasten to Their End"

The glories of our blood and state
   Are shadows, not substantial things;
There is no armour against Fate;
   Death lays his icy hand on kings:
         Sceptre and Crown
         Must tumble down,
And in the dust be equal made
With the poor crooked scythe and spade.

Some men with swords may reap the field,
   And plant fresh laurels where they kill;
But their strong nerves at last must yield;
   They tame but one another still:
         Early or late
         They stoop to fate,
And must give up their murmuring breath
When they, pale captives, creep to death.

The garlands wither on your brow;
   Then boast no more your mighty deeds;
Upon Death's purple altar now
   See where the victor-victim bleeds!
         Your heads must come
         To the cold tomb:
Only the actions of the just
Smell sweet, and blossom in their dust.

JAMES SHIRLEY, 1659.

"Of All Scope Dispossessed"

Laodameia died; Helen died; Leda, the beloved of Jupiter, went before. It is better to repose in the earth betimes than to sit up late; better, than to cling pertinaciously to what we feel crumbling under us, and to protract an inevitable fall. We may enjoy the present while we are insensible of infirmity and decay; but the present, like a note in music, is nothing but as it appertains to what is past and what is to come. There are no fields of amarath on this side of the grave, there are no voices, O Rhodope! that are not soon mute, however tuneful; there is no name, with whatever emphasis of passionate love repeated, of which the echo is not faint at last.

W. S. Landor
Aesop and Rhodope.

Sic Transit . . .

There was another case in which I was concerned, though not as an executor. There the will specified that the executors were to take the ashes out to sea; and some of the residuary legatees decided that they also ought to go, if merely as a mark of respect. On the day appointed, a sou'-wester was blowing. All were horribly seasick. And when at last the ashes were flung out, a gust of contrary wind caught them and blew them back into the faces of the family. All his life the deceased had been of a sardonic and tempestuous disposition, and he lived down to his reputation, even in death.

"So like the old man," the relations said, as they brushed his dust and ashes off their clothes.

Reginald L. Hine
Confessions of an Uncommon Attorney.

[185]

Fear no More

Fear no more the heat o' the Sun,
Nor the furious Winter's rages;
Thou thy worldly task hast done,
Home art gone, and ta'en thy wages.
Golden Lads and Girls all must,
As Chimney-Sweepers, come to dust.

Fear no more the frown o' the Great,
Thou art past the Tyrant's stroke;
Care no more to clothe and eat;
To thee the Reed is as the Oak:
The Sceptre, Learning, Physicke must
All follow this, and come to dust.

Fear no more the Lightning flash,
Nor the all-dreaded Thunder-stone;
Fear not Slander, Censure rash,
Thou hast finish'd joy and moan.
All Lovers young, all Lovers must
Consign to thee, and come to dust. . . .

WILLIAM SHAKESPEARE

Paradise Enow

"When I die," said dear and whimsical old Doctor Pycroft, "I shall have a bell hung on my head-stone, with an inscription asking the compassionate passer-by to ring it long and loud. *And I shan't get up.*"

REGINALD L. HINE
Confessions of an Uncommon Attorney.

The Test of Death

Of all the events which constitute a person's biography, there is scarcely one—none, certainly, of anything like a similar importance—to which the world so easily reconciles itself as to his death. In most other cases and contingencies the individual is present among us, mixed up with the daily revolution of affairs, and affording a definite point for observation. At his decease there is only a vacancy, and a momentary eddy—very small as compared with the apparent magnitude of the ingurgitated object—and a bubble or two, ascending out of the black depth, and bursting at the surface. . . .

It is very singular, how the fact of a man's death often seems to give people a truer idea of his character, whether for good or evil, than they have ever possessed while he was living and acting among them. Death is so genuine a fact that it excludes falsehood, or betrays its emptiness; it is a touchstone that proves the gold, and dishonours the baser metal. Could the departed, whoever he may be, return in a week after his decease, he would almost invariably find himself at a higher or lower point than he had formerly occupied on the scale of public appreciation.

NATHANIEL HAWTHORNE
The House of the Seven Gables.

[187]

Cremation

Scatter my ashes!
Let them be free to the air,
Soaked in the sunlight and rain,
Scatter with never a care
Whether you find them again.
Hereby I make it a trust:
In no grave confined,
Mingle my dust with the dust,
Give me in fee to the wind.
Scatter my ashes!

JOHN GALSWORTHY

The Passing of Mr. Valiant-for-Truth

After this it was noised abroad that Mr. Valiant-for-Truth was taken with a summons by the same post as the other; and had this for a token that the summons was true, "That his pitcher was broken at the fountain" (Eccles. xii, 6). When he understood it, he called for his friends, and told them of it. Then, said he, I am going to my Father's; and though with great difficulty I am got hither, yet now I do not repent me of all the trouble I have been at to arrive where I am. My sword I give to him that shall succeed me in my pilgrimage, and my courage and skill to him that can get it. My marks and scars I carry with me, to be a witness for me, that I have fought His battles who now will be my rewarder. When the day that he must go hence was come, many accompanied him to the river side, into which as he went he said, "Death, where is thy sting?" And as he went down deeper, he said, "Grave, where is thy victory?" So he passed over, and all the trumpets sounded for him on the other side.

JOHN BUNYAN, 1628-1688
The Pilgrim's Progress.

[188]

VI

THE COMPLEAT DOCTOR

" Hippocrates his Oath which he gave unto his disciples and scollers which professing Phisicke and Chirurgerie is very worthie to be observed and kept faithfully "

I swear by Apollo the Healer, and Aesculapius, and Hygieia, and Panacea.

And I call all Gods and Goddesses to witness, that I will, according to my power and judgment, make good this oath, and this covenant which here I sign.

To think of him who taught me this art as I think of my parents. To hold my life as his life, and to give him, in the time of his need, a share of my belongings. To consider his sons as my brothers, and to teach this art, to such of them as wish to learn it, without payment or agreement.

To impart the doctrine, and the interpretation, and the whole learning to my sons, and to my master's sons, and to students enrolled and sworn under medical law, and to nobody else.

And I will use all ways of medical treatment that shall be for the advantage of the sufferers, according to my power and judgment, and will protect them from injury and in-justice. Nor will I give to any man, though I be asked to give it, any deadly drug, nor will I consent that it should be given. Likewise, I will not procure abortion. But purely and holily I will keep guard over my life and my art.

Nor will I cut them that have the stone, but will send them to men whose work it is to perform that operation.

And, into whatever houses I enter, I will enter into them for the benefit of the patients. I will refrain from any wilful hurt or wrong, and from falsehood, and especially from all lewdness, whether it be my chance to deal with men or women, freeman or slave. And, whatever, in practice, I see or hear, or even outside practice, which it is not right should be told abroad, I will be silent, counting as unsaid what was said.

Therefore, as I faithfully observe and keep this my oath, may I have enjoyment in my Art and living, being in good repute among all men for ever and ever: but, if I transgress and break the same, let all things fall out unto me contrary.

" Honest in Thy Preservation "

A good physician comes to thee in the shape of an angel, and therefore let him boldly take thee by the hand, for he has been in God's garden, gathering herbs and sovereign roots to cure thee. The good physician deals in simples and will be simply honest with thee in thy preservation.

THOMAS DEKKER, 1570-1637.

The Good Doctor

He needs to be equipped with tact, resourcefulness, courage, and prudence. He must have patience with fads, considerateness for his patients and their friends, sympathy with suffering, and gentleness of touch and voice. Much indeed is asked of him, but without these qualities, be he never so able, he will make but a poor practitioner.

Sir ARCHIBALD GARROD
B.M.J., 1926.

The Equipment

For the doctor there is needed a kindly heart, a gentle touch, the control to keep a confidence, love of children, with the power to make a decision and to accept responsibility.

T. B. LAYTON
Lancet, 1948.

The Workmen of the Body

Young men, whose pride bruises at a touch, are apt to be offended, when they are thus classed as plumbers and glaziers of the body. Perhaps they have never been seriously ill, never come to that point of sharp thought where the physician, the surgeon, the anaesthetist, are your best friends, your Godsends, not because they talk to you about the National Gallery, but just because they do not talk, but dose, anaesthetise, and incise you. Every doctor, early in his course, ought to stand at that point.

Confessio Medici.

Homo Sum

Make it compulsory for a doctor using a brass plate to have inscribed on it, in addition to the letters indicating his qualifications, the words, "Remember that I, too, am mortal."

GEORGE BERNARD SHAW
Preface to " The Doctor's Dilemma."

The Fascination of Medicine

The public think it strange to hear physicians speak of the fascination which accompanies the study of our art. Literature, painting, and music, do not yield an enjoyment more keen than that which is afforded by the study of medicine, and whoever does not find in it, from the commencement of his career, an almost irresistible attraction, ought to renounce the intention of following our profession.

TROUSSEAU
Lectures on Clinical Medicine.

Sound and Round

A doctor must more than ever before be what Locke calls a "whole, sound, round-about man."

Grains and Scruples
Lancet, 1938.

Faithful Workmen

They maintain the fabric of the world, and in the handiwork of their craft is their prayer.

Apocrypha.

Our Forefathers

To be a good doctor, you must love Medicine. You cannot love it well unless you love also those who have brought it to where it is to-day. Then you realise that in doing your best, you are but paying a debt.

Dr. EDOUARD RIST
Presse Médicale, 1913.

Immortal

The high lights of the profession, from Hippocrates to William Osler, have all left a spirit living in this world. Those medical men and women who have done no more than exchange ideas and work loyally with colleagues need not trouble about their ashes being scattered, for some of their spirit will survive.

Dr. HUGH BARBER
Practitioner, 1948.

A Fine Profession

There is no process which can reckon up the amount of good which the science and art of medicine have conferred upon the human race; there is no moral calculus that can grasp and comprehend the sum of their beneficent operations. Ever since the first dawn of civilisation and learning, through the "dark backward, and abysm of time," they have been the true and constant friends of the suffering sons and daughters of men. Through their ministers and disciples, they have cheered the desponding; they have lightened the load of human sorrow; they have dispelled or diminished the gloom of the sick-chamber; they have plucked from the pillow of pain its thorns, and made the hard couch soft with the poppies of delicious rest; they have let in the light of joy upon dark and desolate dwellings; they have rekindled the lamp of hope in the bosom of despair; they have called back the radiance of the lustreless eye and the bloom of the fading cheek; they have sent new vigour through the failing limbs; and, finally when exhausted in all other resources, and baffled in their skill—handmaids of philosophy and religion—they have blunted the arrows of death, and rendered less rugged and precipitous the inevitable pathway to the tomb. In the circle of human duties, I do not know of any, short of heroic and perilous daring, or religious martyrdom and self-sacrifice, higher and nobler than those of the physician. His daily round of labour is crowded with beneficence, and his nightly sleep is broken, that others may have better rest.

ELISHA BARTLETT
An Inquiry into the Degree of Certainty of Medicine, 1848.

The Happy Life

How happy is he born and taught
That serveth not another's will;
Whose armour is his honest thought,
And simple truth his utmost skill.

Whose passions not his masters are;
Whose soul is still prepared for death,
Untied unto the world by care
Of public fame or private breath;

Who envies none that chance doth raise,
Nor vice; who never understood
How deepest wounds are given by praise;
Nor rules of state, but rules of good.

Who hath his life from rumour freed;
Whose conscience is his strong retreat;
Whose state can neither flatterers feed,
Nor ruin make oppressors great;

Who God doth late and early pray
More of his grace than gifts to lend;
And entertains the harmless day
With a religious book or friend;

—This man is freed from servile bands
Of hope to rise or fear to fall;
Lord of himself, though not of lands,
And having nothing, yet hath all.

Sir HENRY WOOTTON, 1568-1629.

The Doctor as Gentle Man

Good dressing, quiet ways, low tones of voice, lips that can wait, and eyes that do not wander,—shyness of personalities, except in certain intimate communions,—to be *light in hand* in conversation, to have ideas, but to be able to make talk, if necessary, without them,—to belong to the company you are in, and not to yourself,—to have nothing in your dress or furniture so fine that you cannot afford to spoil it and get another like it, yet to preserve the harmonies throughout your person and dwelling: I should say that this was a fair capital of manners to begin with.

OLIVER WENDELL HOLMES
The Professor at the Breakfast-Table.

" Exoteric Qualifications "

Of these exoteric qualifications, some are outward and visible; as a good gentlemanly person, not alarmingly handsome, with an address to suit—that is to say, a genteel self-possession and subdued politeness, not of the very last polish —a slow, low and regular tone of voice, and such an even flow of spirits as neither to be dejected by the sight of pain and the weight of responsibility, nor to offend the anxious and the suffering by an unsympathetic hilarity. The dress should be neat, and rather above than below par in costliness.

In fine, the young physician should carry on something of his profession in his outward man, but yet so that nobody should be able to say what it was.

HARTLEY COLERIDGE
Life of Dr. Fothergill.

Swings and Roundabouts

Physicians of all men are most happy; whatever good success they have the world proclaimeth, and what faults they commit the earth covereth.

> FRANCIS QUARLES
> *Hieroglyphickes of the Life of Man*, 1638.

Compassio Medici

You may be sure that some men, even among those who have chosen the task of pruning their fellow-creatures, grow more and more thoughtful and truly compassionate in the midst of their cruel experience. They become less nervous, but more sympathetic. They have a truer sensibility for others' pain, the more they study pain and disease in the light of science.

> OLIVER WENDELL HOLMES
> *The Professor at the Breakfast-Table.*

Of Work

I don't like work—no man ever does—but I like what is in the work—the chance to find yourself. Your own reality—for yourself, not for others—what no other man can ever know. They can only see the mere show, and never tell what it really means.

> CONRAD
> *The Heart of Darkness.*

Not Your Own

A Scottish country doctor tried to persuade a younger doctor from the life of a general practitioner with the warning "You are just a'body's body."

> *Current story.*

Dedication

When an elderly man looks back upon his early life, he wants to help the young to avoid some of the mistakes which he made himself. My conscience tells me that my own worst fault as a young man was not slackness but over-anxiety about my future—anxiety not so much to win success as to avoid humiliating failure, of which I was never really in much danger. This may have been partly a matter of temperament; but I know now I should have been much happier if I had made just that act of self-dedication which I am pressing upon you. "Show Thou me the way that I should walk in, for I lift up my soul unto Thee. Take me with my faults and capacities, such as they are, and use me as Thou seest fit. Lo, I come to do thy will, O God." When that choice has been made, a man gains an inward peace and serenity which is reflected in his outward demeanour. He can enjoy the little humours of life and take its ups and downs good-naturedly, because he has come to see things in their true proportions. He is not careful and troubled about many things because he knows that most things do not matter very much. Thus to dedicate oneself may be as necessary and salutary for those who are disposed to take life too hard as for those who are naturally disposed to take it too easy.

DEAN INGE
The Gate of Life, 1935.

The Practice of Surgery

Chirurgerie is the quick and ready motion of steadfast hands with experience.

GALEN

[199]

Five Points for the Surgeon

The Chirurgian must also in theis his operations observe five thynges principally. First, that he doeth it safelye, and that wythout hurte or damage to the pacient, secondly, that he do not detracte tyme or let slepe good occasions offered in workyng, but with suche spede as arte wyll soffer, let hym finishe his cure. Therdly, that he work jently, courtyously, and wyth so lytle payne the pacient, as conveniently you may, and not roughly, butcherly, rudlye, and wythout a comlenes. Forthly, that he be as free from crafte and deceyte in all his workynges, as the East is from the Weaste. Fiftly, that he taketh no cure in the hande for lucre or gaynes sake only, but rather for an honest and competent rewarde, with a godly affection, to doe his diligence. Laste of all, that he maketh no warrantyse of suche sicknes, as are incurable, as to cure a Cancer or ulcerate, or elephantiasis confirmed: but circumspectlye to consider what the effecte is, and promyse no more then arte can performe.

Thomas Gale
An Institution of a Chirurgian, 1563.

The Surgeon's Duty

It is the surgeon's duty to tranquillise the temper, to beget cheerfulness and to impart confidence of recovery. Some medical practitioners are so cold and cheerless as to damp every hope; whilst others inspire confidence of recovery and a disregard of situation, which supports the regular performance of all the actions necessary for restoration. It is your duty, therefore, to support hope, to preserve tranquillity, and to inspire cheerfulness, even when you are still doubtful of the issue.

Sir Astley Cooper
Lectures on Surgery, 1824.

[200]

Manners for a Chirurgian

The manners whyche *Guido* woulde have in a Chirurgian are reconed of *Hippocrates and Celsus,* whyche briefelye I wyll numbre: they muste be bolde and wythout feare in suche cures as are with out peryll, and wheras necessitye requireth. Also in cures that be doutful, not to be to raishe and hastie, to be gentle and courtyous towarde the sicke pacient, to be frendlye and lovyng, towarde those of hys profession. Also wyse and circumspecte in Prognostications, last of all, he muste be chaste and temperate of body, mercifull towarde the pore, and not to gredy of mony. And this is sufficient touchynge the description of hym, that muste be admitted in Chirurgerye.

THOMAS GALE
An Institution of a Chirurgian, 1563.

The Surgeon

The guiding circumstance of a surgeon's life is personal responsibility. He is in charge, he must make decisions and initiate or carry out the line of action those decisions imply, and on the correctness of his decisions and the skill and determination with which the action is carried out depends the welfare and possibly the life of the patient. All the material for a correct diagnosis may not be available, at any rate at a particular time, but there must always be a decision; even though it may not be the right one it is the best that can be made at the time and the one on which action must be based if action is needed.

Sir HENEAGE OGILVIE
A Surgeon's Life
Lancet, 1948.

A Fine Endowment

He has the earnest, loving spirit of the real surgeon.

Written by Lister of Thomas Keith of Edinburgh.

[201]

What the Physician Should Be

The physician in modern society holds a very high place. He is generally regarded with respect. It is not merely that his distinctive service is indispensable, and is universally required, but also that he commands the public confidence in a very notable degree, and has behind him a tradition of professional behaviour which is generally admired. It is assumed that he will be adequately trained; that he will be entirely honourable; that he will be patient, considerate and assiduous; that he will be generous and even-minded, giving his service as frankly and fully to the poorest as to the richest of his patients; that he will be, in a quite astonishing measure, disinterested. We expect the doctor to be something more than a scientific specialist, skilled in his specific branch of work. We look for education and good manners. He must be welcome in society for his own sake. No doubt there is a measure of idealising sentiment in this conception of the physician; but it is near enough to general experience to maintain itself in the teeth of all individual contradictions, and its existence is not only a remarkable evidence of the high level of medical professional habit in the modern world, but also a precious possession of the medical profession itself. The Ideal has, of course, never been realised fully in any individual. . . . But the combination in a single picture sets before every medical student a goal which he must strive to reach. That picture was upheld to the physicians of ancient Hellas in the so-called "Hippocratic Oath." It was natural to link it with the name of Hippocrates, for he "will ever remain the type of the perfect physician." . . . It is only,

[202]

however, in modern times that society generally has acknowledged in the medical profession such a standard of professional behaviour as the Hippocratic Oath demands. The brilliant dawn of Greek medical science was soon overcast, and succeeded by the "cloudy and dark day" of superstition and barbarism.

Bishop HENSLEY HENSON
The Genesis of the Physician's Ideal
B.M.J., 1930.

Ideal Physician

There are men and classes of men that stand above the common herd: the soldier, the sailor, and the shepherd not infrequently; the artist rarely; rarelier still the clergyman; the physician almost as a rule. He is the flower (such as it is) of our civilisation; and when that stage of man is done with, and only to be marvelled at in history, he will be thought to have shared as little as any in the defects of the period, and most notably exhibited the virtues of the race. Generosity he has, such as is possible to those who practise an art, never to those who drive a trade; discretion, tested by a hundred secrets; tact, tried in a thousand embarrassments; and what are more important, Heraclean cheerfulness and courage. So that he brings air and cheer into the sick room, and often enough, though not so often as he wishes, brings healing.

R. L. STEVENSON
Underwoods.

The Rewards of Medicine

In all honest work there is ultimate good, but in Medicine the rewards of devotion, of forgetting self in helping the sick and sorrowful, are more immediate; the harvest is gathered on the field. The sense of saving life, or of relieving pain, as promptly as by dragging a drowning man out of the water, is joyful; little grateful as the saved one may be. It is perhaps no less a satisfaction to feel that at least we smooth the pillows and calm the fears of the suffering. And if, in the course of years, these benefits may seem to have been disregarded, and in particular cases they may have been, or if after our English fashion thankful friends have kept an inscrutable silence, yet sooner or later, on some sudden occasion perhaps, their hearts will be opened, and the kindly and skilful physician will find to his comfort that the tokens of the grateful affection of his patients and their friends are poured into his bosom, often from unexpected quarters, in full measure and running over.

Sir CLIFFORD ALLBUTT
Lancet, 1922.

Professional Ethos

I hold every man a debtor to his profession; from which as men of course do seek to receive countenance and profit, so ought they of duty to endeavour themselves, by way of amends, to be a help and ornament thereunto. This is performed, in some degree, by the honest and liberal practice of a profession; where men shall carry a respect not to descend into any course that is corrupt and unworthy thereof, and preserve themselves free from the abuses wherewith the same profession is noted to be infected; but much more is this performed, if a man be able to visit and strengthen the roots and foundation of the science itself; thereby not only gracing it in reputation and dignity, but also amplifying it in profession and substance.

FRANCIS BACON
Essayes.

Imperturbability

Imperturbability means coolness and presence of mind under all circumstances, calmness amid storm, clearness of judgment in moments of great peril, immobility, impassiveness, or, to use an old and expressive word, *phlegm.* It is the quality which is most appreciated by the laity though often misunderstood by them; and the physician who has the misfortune to be without it, who betrays indecision and worry and who shows that he is flustered and flurried in ordinary emergencies, loses rapidly the confidence of his patients. . . .

In a true and perfect form, imperturbability is indissolubly associated with wide experience and an intimate knowledge of the varied aspects of disease. With such advantages he is so equipped that no eventuality can disturb the mental equilibrium of the physician; the possibilities are always manifest, and the course of action clear. From its very nature this precious quality is liable to be misinterpreted, and the general accusation of hardness, so often brought against the profession, has here its foundation. Now a certain measure of insensibility is not only an advantage, but a positive necessity in the exercise of a calm judgment, and in carrying out delicate operations. Keen sensibility is doubtless a virtue of high order, when it does not interfere with steadiness of hand or coolness of nerve; but for the practitioner in his working-day world, a callousness which only thinks of the good to be effected, and goes ahead regardless of smaller considerations, is the preferable quality.

Osler
Aequanimitas, 1889.

The G.P. . . . and Others

General practice is at least as difficult, if it is to be carried on well and successfully, as any special practice can be, and probably more so; for the G.P. has to live continually, as it were, with the results of his handiwork. He is always liable to meet his failures round the next corner; and his mistakes may quite easily rent the pew behind him in the parish church. The consultant, on the other hand, comes into the family life from afar, and returns again, an hour or two later, to the seclusion of his private fastness. He has brought down his little bit of extra technical skill or knowledge. He has used it for good or ill. And the results do not follow him, save indirectly, and at a very comfortable distance. But the G.P. who has taken upon himself the responsibility of calling him in must needs bear upon his shoulders not only the anxiety that heralds ultimate success, but a large share of the possible obloquy that may follow failure.

PETER HARDING, M.D.
The Corner of Harley Street.

Uses of Adversity

Besides, see what you have gained in practice. To be ill, or to undergo an operation, is to be initiated into the mystery of nursing, and to learn the comforts and discomforts of an invalid's life; the unearthly fragrance of tea at daybreak, the disappointment of rice-pudding when you thought it was going to be orange-jelly, and the behaviour of each constituent part of the bedclothes. You know, henceforth, how many hours are in a sleepless night; and what unclean fancies will not let us alone when we are ill; and how illness may blunt anxiety and fear, so that the patient is dull, but not unhappy or worried; and how we cling to life not from

[206]

terror of death, nor with any clear desire for the remainder of life, but by nature, not by logic. In brief, you learn from your own case many facts which are not in text-books and lectures: and your patients, in the years to come, will say that they prefer you to the other doctor, because you seem to understand exactly how they feel. I wish you therefore, young man, early in your career, a serious illness, or an operation, or both.

Confessio Medici.

Open Sesame

Here is an aspect of medicine worth consideration. To the seeing eye and the tender hand there is no easier door into the warm heart of humanity. There is no other profession that will lead you quite so close to reality. And by this I don't mean realism in the modern sense, wherein, as it seems to me, the altogether ugly looms so disproportionately large. For after thirty years of tolerably wide opportunity I have still failed to find the altogether ugly. And though of course you will meet ugliness in plenty—a cancer that will find you shocked, and, alas, largely impotent—yet, if you look long enough, and carefully enough, how often will you discover it to be but the shadow of some clearly shining spiritual beauty. No, you need not fear, I think, to tread behind the veil.

PETER HARDING, M.D.
The Corner of Harley Street.

Unpleasant Work

Public usefulness and the interests of humanity ennoble the most disgusting work.

LAVOISIER, 1743-1794.

The High Calling

The choice lies open, the paths are plain before you. Always seek your own interests, make of a high and sacred calling a sordid business, regard your fellow creatures as so many tools of trade, and, if your heart's desire is for riches, they may be yours; but you will have bartered away the birthright of a noble heritage, traduced the physician's well-deserved title of the Friend of Man, and falsified the best traditions of an ancient and honourable Guild. On the other hand, I have tried to indicate some of the ideals which you may reasonably cherish. No matter though they are paradoxical in comparison with the ordinary conditions in which you work, they will have, if encouraged, an ennobling influence, even if it be for you only to say with Rabbi Ben Ezra, "what I aspired to be and was not, comforts me." And though this course does not necessarily bring position or renown, consistently followed it will at any rate give to your youth an exhilarating zeal and a cheerfulness which will enable you to surmount all obstacles—to your maturity a serene judgment of men and things, and that broad charity without which all else is nought—to your old age that greatest of blessings, peace of mind, a realisation, maybe, of the prayer of Socrates for the beauty in the inward soul and for unity of the outer and the inner man; perhaps the promise of St. Bernard, "pax sine crimine, pax sine turbine, pax sine rixa."

OSLER
Teacher and Student, 1892.

The Scourge of Practice

Consider this instrument of the discipline of practice; that we live under responsibility, and go in fear of making a mistake. In every science and every art, in every business and every trade, mistakes are made: they are a part of all men. But doctors practise their science and their art on life. With that material a mistake may be irreparable. You, who are now a student, keen over your work, and one of the best men of your year at the Hospital, what will you do when that disaster happens? How long will it wait, before it happens? Indeed, it may happen before you leave the Hospital. Say that you are a House-physician or a House-surgeon, hard-worked, sometimes over-worked, careful, gentle, diligent—oh, let us say, and have done with it, that you have every virtue under Heaven—yet the blow may fall, before the end of your term of office, on some man, woman, or child under your care: fall, before your death, on one or more than one of your patients. Look this fact in the face, now, before it comes into your life. People talk of the Fine Arts: but what art is so fine as Medicine, which works in lives, and cannot correct its proofs, or begin with a sketch, or waste its fabrics, or rehearse its effects or use a model; and, by a mistake, injures not an image of life, but life? Why, that is just why Medicine is not fine. It is not the art, but the stuff, which is so fine: we must interfere with that one substance which is above all else in Nature the one texture, man, infinitely complex, infinitely precious. *We touch Heaven*, it is said, *when we lay our hands on the human body*: and the doctor is bound to dose it, to operate on it. This fear of doing harm, which is called the strain of practice, does not pass with the passing of youth; it is acknowledged by a famous surgeon, in a letter written when he was fifty-six. *What happy hours they were*, he says, *of a holiday just over, in their contrast of carelessness with the care of mind with which, here, one goes from one responsibility to another, and always with the thought that, while meaning to do good, one may, from carelessness or inadvertence, do harm.*

Confessio Medici.

Bittersweet

Later, I attended A's son, who died. Nothing could have saved him, I was not at fault, I got another man to see him with me, the treatment was all right, it was a hopeless case from the beginning. All the same, the failure, the dismal going-out of young A, the disappointment were mine: it was I who had to watch him, and to worry myself imagining that I might be doing something better for him. He was my patient, he suffered under me, *passus et sepultus est*; and I heard afterwards that old A said, *The doctor saved me: I wish to God he had saved my boy instead of me.* . . .

You attend a patient, who recovers; and you know that he would have recovered under any doctor as good as you are. You attend a patient, who dies: and you know that he would have died under any doctor; but he died under you. The two events do not balance: the recovery of the one does not sweeten the death of the other. A successful case is like sunshine, or music, or food, which a man enjoys as they come, but they come to everybody: an unsuccessful case is a more intimate experience. *Confessio Medici.*

The Doctor's Pity

On the paper were the words:—"An operation to-day.— J.B. *Clerk.*" Up ran the youths, eager to secure good places: in they crowded, full of interest and talk. "What's the case?" "Which side is it?"

Don't think them heartless; they are neither better nor worse than you or I: they get over their professional horrors, and into their proper work; and in them pity—as an *emotion*, ending in itself or at best in tears and a long drawn breath, lessens, while pity, as a *motive*, is quickened, and gains power and purpose. It is well for poor human nature that it is so.

Dr. JOHN BROWN
Horae Subsecivae, 1861.

" *Abide by the Stuff* "

Foolish people talk as if it were somehow the doctor's fault, and a rebuke against him, that every scrap of his work is saturated with materialism. Why, that is just how he makes it tell. There is no place, in practice, for any other form of thought. Here, for instance, is a patient in immediate danger of death, but not quite past all hope of recovery. To the philosopher, the poet, he is *animula, hospes comesque corporis.* To the doctor who must deal with him at once, and that by methods most unpoetical, he is neither *hospes* nor *comes corporis,* but just *corpus.* We learned him as *corpus* and it took us five years, and some of us more, to learn him that way: and we treat him as *corpus,* because it takes us all our learning to treat him that way. For the sake of our patients, the spirit of practice compels us to work always within the ring-fence of materialism.

Confessio Medici.

The Doctor's Sympathy

The relationship between doctor and patient partakes of a peculiar intimacy. It presupposes on the part of the physician not only knowledge of his fellow men, but sympathy. He sits, not as a judge of morals or of conduct, but rather as an impersonal repository for confession. The patient, on his part, must feel the need of aid, and few patients come to doctors except with this incentive. This aspect of the practice of medicine has been designated as the art; yet I wonder whether it should not, most properly, be called the Essence.

WARFIELD T. LONGCOPE
Methods and Medicine
Bull. Johns Hopkins Hospital, 1932.

Our Reward

Our reward is paid to us part in money and part in kind. We cannot keep separate, as it were in two ledgers, these two incomes: nor can we say exactly at any time, how much we are worth. Our lives are invested in the goodwill of friends, in the confidence of patients, in the approval of the brethren; and in our Hospital record, and in our intention of sticking to work. All these and the like securities are but other names for ourselves. What we are, that we make some of it but not much, in money, and the rest of it in kind.

Confessio Medici.

The Calls of Practice

Lydgate certainly had good reason to reflect on the service his practice did him in counteracting his personal cares. He had no longer free energy enough for spontaneous research and speculative thinking, but by the bedside of patients the direct external calls on his judgment and sympathies brought the added impulse needed to draw him out of himself. It was not simply that beneficent harness of routine which enables silly men to live respectably and unhappy men to live calmly—it was a perpetual claim on the immediate fresh application of thought, and on the consideration of another's need and trial. Many of us looking back through life would say that the kindest man we have ever known has been a medical man, or perhaps that surgeon whose fine tact, directed by deeply-informed perception, has come to us in our need with a more sublime beneficence than that of miracle-workers.

GEORGE ELIOT
Middlemarch.

Fathers and Sons

Especially, a young man must be careful to reckon a successful father not among his assets, but among his liabilities. For he who enters his father's profession counting on his father's name, enters it at his peril: and his venture is the more perilous, if he takes, in the same profession the same line. There was Icarus, son of Daedalus: he fashioned for himself wings, to follow his father aloft; and they bore him off the earth, but the wax of them was melted by the sun, and he fell into the sea. Practice is the solvent of all such things: for it is the man himself, the skill of his hands, the judgment of his reason on the expert evidence of his senses, the quick selection and watchful use of the right set of facts. It cannot be taken over like a theatre-ticket or a share in a railway. Name, influence, privilege, succession, are what we make them.

Confessio Medici.

The Credo *of a Zealous Physician*

I do not say that the study of nature, human and comparative, as far as it relates to medicine, is an easy task; let any one undertake a foreign language, and when he thinks he has mastered it, let him go into its native country and attempt to use it among the polite and well-informed; if he succeed, let him go among the illiterate and rude, where *slang* is current; into the lunatic asylum, where the vernacular is babbled in broken sentences through the mouth of an idiot, and attempt to understand this; should he again succeed he may safely say that he knows that language. Let him then set down and calculate the cost, in labour, time, and talent; then square this amount and go boldly into the study of physiology; and when he has exhausted his programme, he will find himself humbly knocking at the door of the temple, and it will be opened; for diligence, like the vinegar of Hannibal, will make a way through the frozen Alps; it is the *open sesame* of our profession. When he is satisfied with the beautiful proportions of the interior, its vast and varied dimensions, the intricate and astounding action of its machinery, obeying laws of a singular stability, whose very conflict produces harmony under the government of secondary laws—if there is anything secondary in nature!—when he is satisfied (and such are not satisfied until informed), he will be led to his ultimate object, to take his last lessons from the poor and suffering, the fevered and phrenzied, from the Jobs and Lazaruses—into the pesthouses and prisons, and here, in these magazines of misery and contagion, these Babels of disease and sin, he must not only take up his abode, but following the example of his Divine Master, he must love to dwell there—this is Pathology.

When such a one re-enters the world, he is a physician; his vast labours have not only taught him how little he knows, but that he knows this little well. Conscious of this virtue, he feels no necessity of trumpeting his professional acquirements abroad, but with becoming modesty and true dignity, which constitute genuine professional pride, he leaves this to the good sense of his fellow citizens to discover.

JOHN BASSETT
Quoted by Osler in "An Alabama Student."

Different Sorts

There are seueral sorts of physicians 1st. some yt canne talke but doe nothing; 2ly some yt canne doe but not talke; 3rdly some yt canne both doe and talk; 4thly some yt canne neither doe nor talk and these get most money.

REV. JOHN WARD

Of Hym that shall Learne Physicke

Tho. Gale: Who so ever (sayth Hippocrates) wyll learne the arte of Physicke, folowyng these guides he shal have hys desire. Nature, learnyng, an apte place for stodye, good bryngyng uppe from the chyldhoode, diligence, and tyme. For fyrst of all nature is to be looked for. For nature repugnynge, all thinges are frustrat. But yf that nature be inclyned unto the best thynges, the knoweledge of the arte wyll easely folowe, whyche it behoveth to get throughe prudence, so that from the chyldehoode he be well trayned uppe, and that in a place apte for stodye, further more he muste bestowe great dilygence, and that for a longe tyme, so that learnynge (beynge nowe grafted in hym) maye happelye, and that wyth increase brynge forthe her fruites. And Hippocrates resembleth the stody of Phisycke unto agriculture or tyllage, For (saythe he) what consyderation is of those thynges whyche the earth bryngeth out, the lyke in all poyntes is of the knowledge of Phisycke. For our nature is as it ware the fielde, the disciplynes of teachers are like the seades; also the institution and bringynge up from the childhode, is resembled to the castynge of seade into the grounde in dewe and convenient tyme, the place in whyche he must learne, is as it were the ayre gyvinge norishment to suche thyngs as sprynge oute of the grounde. The industrie and diligence bestowed in the art, is lyke the tyllage of the plowman, and laste of all, tyme dothe strenthen these, and suffereth them perfectlye to be norished.

THOMAS GALE
An Institution of a Chirurgian, 1563.

The Choice of a Physician

Physicians are some of them so pleasing, and conformable to the Humor of the Patient, as they presse not the true cure of the Disease; and some other are so Regular, in proceeding according to Art, for the Disease, as they respect not sufficiently the Condition of the Patient. Take one of a Middle Temper; Or if it may not be found in one Man, combine two of either sort: And forget not to call, as well the best acquainted with your Body, as the best reputed of for his Faculty.

Francis Bacon
Essayes.

Cheerfulness and Serenity

If you are making choice of a physician, be sure you get one, if possible, with a cheerful and serene countenance. A physician is not—at least, ought not to be—an executioner; and a sentence of death on his face is as bad as a warrant for execution signed by the Governor. As a general rule, no man has a right to tell another by word or look that he is going to die. It may be necessary in some extreme cases; but as a rule, it is the last extreme of impertinence which one human being can offer to another. "You have killed me," said a patient once to a physician who had rashly told him he was incurable. He ought to have lived six months but he was dead in six weeks. If we will only let nature and the God of Nature alone, persons will commonly learn their condition, as early as they ought to know it, and not be cheated out of their natural birthright of hope of recovery, which is intended to accompany sick people as long as life is comfortable, and is graciously replaced by the hope of heaven, or at least of rest, when life has become a burden which the bearer is ready to let fall.

Oliver Wendell Holmes
The Professor at the Breakfast-Table.

The Bubble Reputation

A physician seems to be the mere plaything of fortune; his degree of reputation is for the most part totally casual; they that employ him know not his excellence; they that reject him know not his deficiency.

SAMUEL JOHNSON
Life of Mark Akenside.

" What is Lost on the Swings . . ."

I have often remarked that, though a physician is sometimes blamed very unjustly, it is quite as common for him to get more credit than he is fairly entitled to; so that he has not, on the whole, any right to complain.

JAMES JACKSON, M.D.
Letters to a Young Physician, 1855.

The Right Mood

In all our doings we must spend our lives in truth, faith, hope, love—clinging to that mood of mind, bent on winning to the very heart of everything; believing in real work as the means whereby in its own good time what is now hidden will be laid bare; trusting that the end of our quest will be the furtherance of knowledge and the good of mankind; and holding each of our fellow workers in such kindly thought as will lead us to be happy when any of them makes a forward step. May each of us be able to say in the words of a historical rascal, who yet had the elements of good in him, François Villon:—"En ceste foy je veuil vivre et mourir."

G. A. GIBSON, M.D.
Montreal Medical Journal, 1908.

[217]

A Moment of Initiation

                    Magnificent
    The morning was, in memorable pomp,
    More glorious than I ever had beheld.
    The Sea was laughing at a distance; all
    The solid Mountains were as bright as clouds,
    Grain-tinctured, drench'd in empyrean light;
    And in the meadows and the lower grounds
    Was all the sweetness of a common dawn,
    Dews, vapours, and the melody of birds,
    And Labourers going forth into the fields.
    Ah! need I say, dear Friend, that to the brim
    My heart was full; I made no vows, but vows
    Were then made for me; bond unknown to me
    Was given that I should be, else sinning greatly,
    A dedicated Spirit. On I walked
    In blessedness, which even yet remains.

                                        WORDSWORTH
                                        The Prelude.

The Kindling of Vocation

Most of us who turn to any subject with love remember some morning or evening when we got on a high stool to reach down an untried volume, or sat with parted lips listening to a new talker, or for very lack of books began to listen to the voices within, as the first traceable beginning of our love.

One vacation, a wet day sent him to the small home library to hunt once more for a book which might have some freshness for him: in vain! unless, indeed, he took down the dusty row of volumes with grey-paper backs and dingy labels—the volumes of an old Cyclopaedia which he had never disturbed. It would at least be a novelty to disturb them. They were on the highest shelf, and he stood on a chair to get them down. But he opened the volume which he first took from the shelf; somehow, one is apt to read in a makeshift attitude, just where it might seem inconvenient to do so. The page he opened on was under the head of Anatomy, and the first passage that drew his eyes was on the valves of the heart. He was not much acquainted with valves of any sort, but he knew that valvae were folding-doors, and through this crevice came a sudden light startling him with his first vivid notion of finely-adjusted mechanism in the human frame. A liberal education had of course left him free to read the indecent passages in the school classics, but beyond a general sense of secrecy and obscenity in connection with his internal structure, had left his imagination quite unbiassed, so that for anything he knew his brains lay in small bags at his temples, and he had no more thought of representing to himself how his blood circulated than how paper served instead of gold. But the moment of vocation had come, and before he got down from his chair, the world was made new to him by a presentiment of endless processes filling the vast spaces planked out of his sight by that wordy ignorance which he had supposed to be knowledge. From that hour Lydgate felt the growth of an intellectual passion.

GEORGE ELIOT
Middlemarch.

Hospice

Here at whatever hour you come, you will find light and help and human kindness.

> (*Inscription on the lamp to light his patients to the hospital quay when coming down the river to Dr. Albert Schweitzer's hospital at Lambarene.*)

The Daily Round of Hospital

To a young man of good disposition, tired of the preliminary sciences, and of humanity stated in terms of anatomy and physiology to the satisfaction of the examiners, this plunge into the actual flood of lives is a fine experience. Hitherto, he has learned organisms; now, he begins to learn lives. He need not go, like other young men, for that lesson, to the slums: for they come to him, and that thrilling drama, How THE POOR LIVE, is played to him, daily, by the entire company, hero and heroine, villain and victim, comic relief, scenic effects, and a great crowd of supers at the back of the stage—undesired babies, weedy little boys and girls, hooligans, consumptive workpeople, unintelligible foreigners, voluble ladies, old folk of diverse temperaments, and many, too many, more comfortable but not more interesting people. It all happens so naturally, with such a quick and sure touch: the reality of the day's work, the primal meaning of the crowd, the clash of hand-to-hand encounter with disease and injuries, urge him to unexpected uses of himself. Here are the very people of the streets, whom he passes every day, here they are coming to him for help, to him of all men, telling him all about it, how it happened, what it feels like, why they did it: looking to him, right away, for advice and physic. They are no two of them alike: and their records, laid before him, range through every intermediate shade from purest white to a nauseating black. He begins to see that he has more to learn than the use of a stethoscope: he must learn lives.

Confessio Medici.

Hospital

A visitor, loitering here, will see that we are a brotherhood, and that the patients are our guests. Every Hospital is a charity; but there is a difference between charity and hospitality. They who give money to Hospitals, are charitable; we, who have the spending of it are hospitable: and, of course, it is we who get the fun out of the money. And we spend it well, entertaining in good style our innumerable guests.

Confessio Medici.

Hospital

What wonder, then, that many, sore let and hindered in running the race, fall by the way, and need a shelter in which to recruit or to die, in which there shall be no harsh comments on conduct, but only, so far as is possible, love and peace and rest? Here, we learn to scan gently our brother man, judging not, asking no questions, but meting out to all alike a hospitality worthy of the *Hôtel-Dieu*, and deeming ourselves honoured in being allowed to act as its dispensers. Here, too, are daily before our eyes the problems which have ever perplexed the human mind; problems not presented in the dead abstract of books, but in the living concrete of some poor fellow in his last round, fighting a brave fight, but sadly weighted, and going to his account "unhousel'd, disappointed, unanel'd, no reckoning made." As we whisper to each other over his bed that the battle is decided and Euthanasia alone remains, have I not heard in reply to that muttered proverb, so often on the lips of the physician, "the fathers have eaten sour grapes," your answer, in clear accents —the comforting words of the prayer of Stephen?

OSLER
Doctor and Nurse, 1891.

[221]

Hobbies

Keep an hour or two now and then for the cultivation of at least one hobby. And by "hobby" I do not mean a form of athletic recreation, but some pursuit which engages your interest and involves a certain amount of intellectual activity. It should be completely divorced from your professional studies, and if possible should lead you into association with men and women whose vocations and outlooks are different from your own.   Sir FARQUHAR BUZZARD
                                                Lancet, 1933.

Holidays

I don't want you to curtail your holidays. I have far too much respect both for holidays in general and yourself in particular. For it's one of the most pathetic features about the genuine old codger (and one of his surest signs too) that his periods of recreation tend to become progressively shorter —and not always by force of circumstances. They may actually begin to bore him. He may even have to make an effort of will to prolong them for his ultimate good—to school himself into regarding them as cures. Thus, while at twenty-two a summer vacation of less than two months is too monstrous to be seriously considered, at forty-two one becomes grateful for a fortnight, could do with three weeks, but is apt to find a month just a trifle too long. Whereas at fifty-two——. So don't curtail them. And yet better is it to curtail them than to pollute. And unless you particularly need them for preserving specimens of the local flora or maintaining the creases upon your Sunday trousers, you should never, never, never pack technical books in a holiday trunk. It is to put poison—or at any rate water—into the wine that you are to pour out before the gods of mountain and moor and loch.   PETER HARDING, M.D.
                                        The Corner of Harley Street.

[222]

Samuel Johnson Gives Advice on Holidays

Dear Sir,

I am much pleased that you are going a very long journey, which may by proper conduct restore your health and prolong your life.

Observe these rules:

1. Turn all care out of your head as soon as you mount the chaise.

2. Do not think of frugality; your health is worth more than it can cost.

3. Do not continue any day's journey to fatigue.

4. Take now and then a day's rest.

5. Get a smart sea-sickness, if you can.

6. Cast away all anxiety, and keep your mind easy.

This last direction is the principal; with an unquiet mind, neither exercise, nor diet, nor physick can be of much use.

I wish you, dear Sir, a prosperous journey and a happy recovery.

>   I am, dear sir,
>
>   Your most affectionate, humble servant,
>
>   Sam. Johnson.

July 28, 1782.

BOSWELL
Life of Johnson.

Holidays

Sir James Paget (1814-1899) did without a real holiday for fifteen years (1845-1860) during his hard struggle as a young surgeon-pathologist; this, of course, was long before he "learned the misery of making only £4,000 a year."

Sir Henry Holland (1788-1873), whose span of life was the same, early determined never to allow his income from practice to exceed £5,000 a year, and to spend two months every year in travel; this he did for nearly sixty years (1814-1873).

Sir HUMPHRY ROLLESTON
Lancet, 1925.

Of Courtesy Calls

It is not only rational but essential for a doctor settling in a new place to call on the other doctors there because he is going to be one of them. And he should make himself known as agreeably as possible, not as if he expected them to hand over their practices, but as one man talking to others in as modest a way as possible, not boasting of his advantages or ability in any particular line, or the advance of medicine in which he has participated, because after all those things smack of the freshman, no matter how true they seem. And from the very beginning you should get on good and friendly terms with the other doctors. That is very often not done, and always with unfortunate results. People working in the same profession ought to work together; if any man from the beginning makes up his mind that he is going to be friendly and forbearing rather than otherwise, things will be very much better.

GEORGE DOCK
Medical Ethics and Etiquette, 1906.

A Pleasant Testimonial

Dear Sir,

The gentleman who waits on you with this is Mr. Cruikshank, who wishes to succeed his friend Dr. Hunter as professor of Anatomy in the Royal Academy. His qualifications are very generally known, and it adds dignity to the Institution that such men are Candidates.

I am, Sir,

Your most humble Servant,

Samuel Johnson.

To Sir Joshua Reynolds.

"*Young Man, Beware! Likewise Take Care . . .*"

But the young doctor, the new doctor, in a gossipy house, must never be off his guard. He has seen and prescribed for his patient, and has said all that need be said to the friends; and there is tea, and what seems a favourable opportunity for extending the practice. Trust them not, young man: put your fingers in your ears, and flee from the City of Destruction of Reputations. If you must stay, do not stay long, and keep the door of your lips. Talk of the patient, of the weather, or of the proposition, which will as surely as the bread-and-butter be handed to you, that *There is a good deal of illness about.* Avoid all topics of Church and State, quote neither poetry nor prose, give neither censure nor approval to music and the drama, hiding your liking for any art but your own. Leave behind you, for gossip to lap, a saucerful of the milk of human kindness. Never mind about producing a favourable impression; produce this one impression, that you know your work, and that it will not be your fault if the mixture fails to relieve the patient upstairs: and then flee.

Confessio Medici.

How to Get On

Have the carriage out the whole day, whether you are in it or not. . . . The late Mr. Heaviside always contended that his cream-coloured carriage, picked out with sky-blue, and a pair of grey horses, hooked many a patient for him, as everybody knew the vehicle, it was so conspicuous.

When you can manage it, let your carriage stand as often and as long as possible at the doors of distinguished characters, such as Bishops, and men of power—men filling the highest offices of state. . . .

Intercepted Letters
Lancet, 1833.

The Delilah of the Press

In the life of every successful physician there comes the temptation to toy with the Delilah of the press—daily and otherwise. There are times when she may be courted with satisfaction, but beware! sooner or later she is sure to play the harlot, and has left many a man shorn of his strength, namely, the confidence of his professional brethren. Not altogether with justice have some notable members of our profession laboured under the accusation of pandering too much to the public. When a man reaches the climacteric, and has long passed beyond the professional stage of his reputation we who are still "in the ring" must exercise a good deal of charity, and discount largely the *on dits* which indiscreet friends circulate. It cannot be denied that in dealings with the public just a little touch of humbug is immensely effective, but it is not necessary. In a large city there were three eminent consultants of world-wide reputation; one was said to be a good physician but no humbug, the second was no physician but a great humbug, the third was a great physician and a great humbug. The first achieved the greatest success, professional and social, possibly not financial.

OSLER
Internal Medicine as a Vocation, 1897.

Success

In a play of Oscar Wilde's one of the characters remarks, "there are only two great tragedies in life, not getting what you want—and getting it!" and I have known consultants whose treadmill life illustrated the bitterness of this *mot*, and whose great success at sixty did not bring the comfort they had anticipated at forty. The mournful echo of the words of the preacher rings in their ears, words which I not long ago heard quoted with deep feeling by a distinguished physician, "Better is a handful with quietness, than both the hands full with travail and vexation of spirit."

OSLER
Internal Medicine as a Vocation, 1897.

" There is no Health in Them "

There is a dishonour in being overcome by the love of money, or of wealth, or of political power, whether a man is frightened into surrender by the loss of them, or, having experienced the benefits of money and political corruption, is unable to rise above the seductions of them. For none of these things are of a permanent or lasting nature; not to mention that no generous friendship ever sprang from them.

PLATO
Symposium.

Self Revelation

To write an article of any sort, is, to some extent, to reveal ourselves. Hence, even a medical article is, in a sense, something of an autobiography.

JOHN CHALMERS DA COSTA
Selected Papers and Speeches, 1931.

[227]

Dishonest Books

Never read any book that bears internal marks of being addressed more to the public than to the profession. They are all bad, and many dishonest.

Dr. PETER MERE LATHAM
Lectures on Clinical Medicine, 1836.

Limelight

You can always avoid the limelight if you try.

WILFRED TROTTER

Cacoethes Scribendi

As a rule disease as it stalks through the land cannot keep pace with the incurable vice of scribbling about it.

JOHN MAYOU
de Rachitide, 1668.

Natural Causes

Some years ago I wrote to a country practitioner to ascertain the end-results of cases of gastrectomy. I explained to him that the information was needed to compare the results from Dublin, with those of other countries, at an annual meeting of the British Medical Association. His reply, dictated more by patriotism than accuracy, indicated that the patients were well in every respect when last he saw them, but that in some mysterious manner they had disappeared one by one from the district. He added that as the country was disturbed they must have been shot, "or died from other natural causes."

DE COURCY WHEELER
Pillars of Surgery
S.G.O., 1933.

The Doctor as a Minister of Justice

The general attitude of the law towards the medical man is to treat him, not as an advocate or as one supporting a particular thesis for its own sake, but as himself a minister of justice, anxious to assist the court at arriving at a true conclusion. To doctors who are called upon to give evidence, I would say that it is of the first importance for them to make sure whether they are speaking of something which they have ascertained as a fact, or are simply putting before the court their impression or theory.

LORD ATKIN
Middlesex Hospital Medical Society, 1925.

Medical Witness

If you make a deduction from certain stated facts, be quite sure that there is no flaw in your deduction. No less a person than a very learned judge whose face was an exact counterpart of that of George III on the coins, on one occasion when counsel was inviting a jury to infer a certain consequence from the likeness of two people to each other, interrupted him, saying, "Don't dwell too long on that. It has been said I am the son of His late Majesty George II because of my likeness to him; all I can say upon that subject is this: George III was never in Scotland, and my mother was never out of it; so if you can make me out to be his son, do. Now go on." Counsel, in a stage whisper for the jury to hear, to his neighbour: "But they might have met at the border!"

H. H. JOY, K.C.
The Medical Witness
B.M.J., 1925.

How not to do it

In a case before a judge and jury a doctor stated in his evidence that on examining the plaintiff he found him suffering from "a severe contusion of the integuments under the left orbit, with great extravasation of blood and ecchymosis in the surrounding cellular tissue which was in a tumefied state; there was also considerable abrasion of the cuticle." The judge: "I suppose you mean that he had a black eye?" The doctor: "Yes." The judge: "Then why not say so."

H. H. JOY, K.C.
The Medical Witness
B.M.J., 1925.

Doctor and Patient

The relation of doctor and patient, from which medical science and practice arise, conditions everything within the field of medicine and is itself conditioned by the nature of human relations in general. The patient is a person who is anxious about himself, who asks another person to help him. The fact that the doctor-patient relation is a relation of persons provides certain principles in itself. Just as a teacher who teaches his subject and not his pupils is a bad teacher, so a doctor who sets out to heal diseases instead of healing people will not be a good doctor. The patient as a person requiring help is the focus of all problems in medicine. If medicine treats diseases, then a classification of diseases into bodily and mental will arise in which the unity of the person is lost sight of. Physicians and psychotherapists will have different objects to treat, and the necessity of co-operation in treating a patient who is always suffering in mind, whether or not he is suffering organically, will be lost sight of. Every case which a doctor deals with arises because of the patient's anxiety about himself. His anxiety, which brings him to the doctor, is his sense that something is the matter with him. The task of the physician is to discover what is the matter. If some malfunctioning of the organism can be discovered, then it can be correlated with the anxiety of the patient about himself. If this is correct then the restoration of proper bodily functioning will remove this anxiety and bring the relation of doctor and patient to an end. But if the doctor can assure himself that there is no organic failure sufficient to account for the anxiety of the patient, what is to be done? The physician may feel inclined to say that there is nothing the matter with him. But there must be something the matter with a man who comes to a doctor when there is nothing the matter with him. The anxiety must have a cause. As it is an anxiety about himself the cause must lie in himself. If it has no observable bodily correlate, the anxiety itself is a disease, and expresses the patient's sense that something is the matter with his functioning as a human being.

Professor JOHN MACMURRAY
A Philosopher's view of Modern Psychology
Lancet, 1938.

" Neither Jew nor Greek . . ."

In 1832, in the riots in Paris, the prefect of police enjoined the doctors of hospitals to point out the rioters who were under their care: the duty of the doctor in such a case is dictated by the noble answer of Dupytren—"qu'il ne voyait point des insurgés, mais seulement des blessés."

ACHARD
Le Premier Libre de Médecine.

[231]

" Who Needs Me is My Neighbour "

A teacher of the law stood up to test Jesus with a question. "Teacher," said he, "what shall I do to inherit eternal life?" "What is written in the Law," replied Jesus, "what do you read there?" He answered: "Thou shalt love the Lord thy God with all thy heart, and with all thy soul, and with all thy strength, and with all thy mind; and thy neighbour as thyself." "Quite right," said Jesus, "do it, and you shall live." But desiring to justify himself, he said to Jesus, "Ah, but who is my neighbour?" Jesus replied:

"Once upon a time there was a man on his way down from Jerusalem to Jericho; and he fell among robbers, who stripped him of his clothes and beat him, and then went off, leaving him half dead. Now a certain priest chanced to be going down that road, but when he saw the man, he passed by on the other side. Likewise a Levite came to the same spot, and seeing him, he too passed by on the other side. However, a Samaritan who was travelling along came to where the man lay, and when he saw him, was moved with pity. He went over to him, and bound up his wounds, dressing them with oil and wine, and he set him on his own mule, and took him to an inn, and took care of him. The next morning he took out some money and handed it to the inn-keeper, and said, 'Look after him, and if you are put to more expense I will repay you when I come back.'

Now tell me, which of these three men proved neighbour to the man who fell among the robbers?"

> *St. Luke* x. 25-36.
> (*It was somewhat as though the victim, the priest and the Levite were Ulstermen on their way to Belfast, and the Samaritan a Sinn Feiner—or vice versa.*)

Mother and Child

I recollect a visit to the cottage of a rural labourer. I see now, strapped to a chair in the garden, a repulsive form with enormous head and stunted limbs, speechless, helpless as a new-born babe, a youth of 14 years, idiot from birth. I hear now the mother's anxious query, "Have you come to take him away?" and her quick addition, with hand uplifted in emphasis, "Sir, I would not part with that child, though you gave me all between earth and sky."

Dr. J. PEARSE
Personal Retrospect of General Practice
Lancet, 1919.

St. Paul on Charity

Though I speak with the tongues of men and of angels, and have not charity, I am become as sounding brass, or a tinkling cymbal. And though I have the gift of prophecy, and understand all mysteries, and all knowledge; and though I have all faith, so that I could remove mountains, and have not charity, I am nothing. And though I bestow all my goods to feed the poor, and though I give my body to be burned, and have not charity, it profiteth me nothing. Charity suffereth long, and is kind; charity envieth not; charity vaunteth not itself, is not puffed up, doth not behave itself unseemly, seeketh not her own, is not easily provoked, thinketh no evil, rejoiceth not in iniquity, but rejoiceth in the truth; beareth all things, believeth all things, hopeth all things, endureth all things. Charity never faileth.

First Epistle to the Corinthians, xiii.

The Mixed Stuff of Life

Amid an eternal heritage of sorrow and suffering our work is laid, and this eternal note of sadness would be insupportable if the daily tragedies were not relieved by the spectacle of the heroism and devotion displayed by the actors. Nothing will sustain you more potently than the power to recognise in your humdrum routine, as perhaps it may be thought, the true poetry of life—the poetry of the commonplace, of the ordinary man, of the plain, toil-worn woman, with their loves and their joys, their sorrows and their griefs. The comedy, too, of life will be spread before you, and nobody laughs more often than the doctor at the pranks Puck plays upon the Titanias and the Bottoms among his patients. The humorous side is really almost as frequently turned towards him as the tragic. Lift up one hand to heaven and thank your stars if they have given you the proper sense to enable you to appreciate the inconceivably droll situations in which we catch our fellow creatures. Unhappily, this is one of the free gifts of the gods, unevenly distributed, not bestowed on all, or on all in equal portions. In undue measure it is not without risk, and in any case in the doctor it is better appreciated by the eye than expressed on the tongue.

OSLER
The Student Life, 1905.

Loyal Support

There was a man who had a large family, and he had never paid his doctor a penny. On one occasion when the doctor hinted that his financial obligations were neglected, the man replied: "Well, I can say, Doctor, you have always had my loyal and devoted support."

Professor GREY TURNER, *at a farewell dinner.*

[234]

What the Public Wants

The demands of this poor public are not reasonable, but they are quite simple. It dreads disease and desires to be protected against it. But it is poor, and wants to be protected cheaply. Scientific measures are too hard to understand, too costly, too clearly tending towards a rise in the rates and more public interference with the insanitary, because insufficiently financed, private house. What the public wants, therefore, is a cheap magic charm to prevent, and a cheap pill or potion to cure all disease. It forces all such charms on the doctors.

GEORGE BERNARD SHAW
Preface to " The Doctor's Dilemma."

A Word to Patients

I have once seen the Man that dyed to save Charges. What! Give Ten Shillings to a Doctor, and have an Apothecary's Bill besides, that may come to I know not what! No, not he: Valuing Life less than Twenty Shillings. But indeed such a Man could not well set too low a Price upon himself: who, though he liv'd up to the Chin in Bags, had rather dye than find in his Heart to open one of them to save his Life.

Such a Man is felo de se, and deserves not Christian Burial.

WILLIAM PENN
Fruits of Solitude.

Compassion

Blest is the man whose bowels move
And melt with pity for the poor . . .
He in the time of greatest need
Shall find the Lord has bowels too.

DR. ISAAC WATTS

Our Patients

Curious, odd compounds are these fellow-creatures, at whose mercy you will be; full of fads and eccentricities, of whims and fancies; but the more closely we study their little foibles of one sort or another in the inner life which we see, the more surely is the conviction borne in upon us of the likeness of their weaknesses to our own. The similarity would be intolerable, if a happy egotism did not often render us forgetful of it. Hence the need of an infinite patience and of an ever-tender charity towards these fellow-creatures; have they not to exercise the same toward us?

OSLER
Aequanimitas, 1889.

Conversing with the Patient and his Friends

To a sick man his doctor's visit is the chief event of the day. Cardiac patients react quickly to the atmosphere surrounding them; they must be helped to keep or gather courage. Cardiac cases are naturally sanguine; depression, when it comes, usually derives from others. It is the doctor's plain duty to enter the sick-room with cheerfulness, to give counsel thoughtfully but confidently, and to leave behind as he goes an appropriate word of encouragement, to comfort the patient in his waiting, to help his suffering, or to allay his fears. A countenance of gloom is as out of place in a sick-room as is a coffin.

In speaking with a patient or his friend about the nature of the malady, truth of statement is a first essential. It is not always expedient to volunteer the whole truth; but answers must be given to direct questions; evasions usually defeat their purpose. When a man in his right mind demands to know if he is dying, as seldomly he does, he should have his answer; and if it is definitely adverse, it can be conveyed compassionately. Spontaneously to acquaint a patient that his life is in grave danger is rarely necessary or advisable. It sometimes becomes desirable to convey to him, directly or through his family or legal adviser, that it would be a simple act of wisdom if he set his house in order.

To patient or to patient's friend simple and unmistakable language should be used; veiled statements are too apt to be misinterpreted. The words must be chosen thoughtfully. The word "disease" should never be used; disease of the heart conveys at once to most patients the idea of something incurable and threatening. The language should be as untechnical as it can be made. A patient has a right to be told what ails him, if he so desires, in terms that convey an idea of the magnitude and significance of the trouble; he has no right to technical diagnostic terms, and it is very rarely wise to parade these before him. Accurate information cannot be conveyed by means of strange words, which to unaccustomed ears bring unintended meanings; and for many the word once caught up becomes a matter requiring search in medical books, or a topic of debate with other patients. Thus the word "angina" should never come first from a doctor, if it is understood at all it will convey in almost all instances an ominous meaning; yet the prognosis varies up to fifteen years. The word "dropsy" is to be avoided, and the adjective "malignant" eliminated completely from the medical man's vocabulary. The valves should not be named, nor murmurs mentioned. These names and details should be of no concern to patients. Methods of examination likewise require little or no explanation; a clear example of the unhappy effects of unnecessarily disclosing technical detail is the well-known instance of high blood-pressure readings.

Sir THOMAS LEWIS
Diseases of the Heart.

Fools and Their Fatness

(i) His bulk caused Joseph Sedley much anxious thought and alarm; now and then he would make a desperate attempt to get rid of his superabundant fat; but his indolence and love of good living speedily got the better of these endeavours at reform, and he found himself again at his three meals a day. He never was well dressed; but he took the hugest pains to adorn his big person, and passed many hours daily in that occupation. His valet made a fortune out of his wardrobe: his toilet table was covered with as many pomatums and essences as ever were employed by an old beauty: he had tried, in order to give himself a waist, every girth, stay, and waistband then invented. Like most fat men, he *would* have his clothes made too tight, and took care they should be of the most brilliant colours and youthful cut.

THACKERAY
Vanity Fair.

(ii) Time and feeding had expanded that once romantic form; the black silk waistcoat had become more and more developed; inch by inch had the gold watch-chain beneath it disappeared from the range of Tupman's vision, and gradually had the capacious chin encroached upon the borders of the white cravat; but the soul of Tupman had known no change—admiration of the fair sex was still its ruling passion.

DICKENS
Pickwick Papers.

When We Are Ill

> This is the way physicians mend or end us,
> *Secundum artem*; but although we sneer
> In health—when ill, we call them to attend us,
> Without the least propensity to jeer;
> While that *hiatus maxime deflendus*
> To be fill'd up by spade or mattock, 's near,
> Instead of gliding graciously down Lethe,
> We tease mild Baillie, or soft Abernethy.   BYRON

A Parable about a Tiresome Patient

An aged man, whom Abraham hospitably invited to his tent, refused to join him in prayer to the one spiritual God. Learning that he was a fire-worshipper, Abraham drove him from his door. That night God appeared to Abraham in a vision and said: "I have borne with that ignorant man for seventy years: could you not have patiently suffered him one night?"   *The Talmud.*

National Milk

Will you please send form for cheap milk. I have a baby two months old and did not know anything about it until a friend told me.

Please send me form for supply of milk for having children at reduced rate.

I have a baby 18 months old, thanking you for same.

Milk is wanted for the baby and Father is unable to supply it.

Prescription as Before

The old school caretaker had grown conversational. "Ah dain't howd wi doctors, Ah dain't. But, mind, them as cuts ye up is all right. Th' owd woman had a kidney oot thirty years ago an' she'd been grand iver sin. She's a bit off colour now, though." After a pause to think this out, he continued, "Ah think Ah'll hev her other kidney takken oot as well." The Countryman, 1949.

Born to Blush Unseen

Blatant utility is no royal road to fame, as improvements in medicine show. I do not suppose that any drug has communicated much more to human happiness than aspirin; there are many which are more indispensable and do much more to save life, but from the consumer's point of view there are very few that are of so much use to him in getting through the changes and chances of his life. But I have no idea of the name of the man who brought it into use (which may of course be just ignorance), and Einstein is better known to the general body of people who eat it. Nor is aspirin celebrated when orations are made about the progress of medicine.

A RUSTICATING PATHOLOGIST
Grains and Scruples
Lancet, 1937.

The Bad Old Days

The Hôtel-Dieu in Paris, like all other hospitals, became a hot-bed of sepsis; and it was remarked that the inscription over its doors "This is the house of God and the gate of Heaven" was more literally true than its founders appreciated.

Sir CHARLES BALLANCE
Remarks and Reminiscences
B.M.J., 1927.

Pensions

I am forwarding my marriage certificate and two children, one which is a mistake, as you will see.

Please find out if my husband is dead as the man I am now living with won't eat or do anything until he is sure.

Please send my money at once, as I have fallen into errors with my Landlord.

I have no children as my husband is a bus conductor and works all day and night.

I want money quick as you can send it. I have been in bed with the doctor for a week and it has not done me any good.

Sir, I am glad to inform you that my husband that was previously reported missing is now dead.

Euthanasia

What of the relations between medicine and the deliberate termination of life? The subject of Euthanasia is an old and a recurring one. We are likely to hear more of it in the immediate future. To many who discuss it the problem seems simple, but to us who are brought in daily contact with the facts there is perhaps no problem more difficult. Whose life should be terminated? And by whose decision? At what level of congenital defects, whether physical or mental, should the cleavage come? What diseases are to be regarded as incurable and at what stages in them should the cup of Lethe be drunk? Is the patient's judgment to be relied upon, warped as it so often is, whether by his malady or by his treatment? How can we know that his mood is permanent? So few moods are. More subtle still is that need to distinguish between the calculated decision of a man's intelligence and the cry of strained emotion for relief. An exhortation to preserve his morale, to play the man, the force of our own personality in enabling him to win through—these are not the least of our functions as doctors. They are based upon an old-fashioned virtue, but nature has provided no other by which the last enemy may be faced. It remains to be seen if we are to be asked to relieve some of our patients of this grim fight altogether. Meantime we must go through with this, the hardest of all our tasks, with patience and with resource, even though we get no gratitude:

> ". . . he hates him
> That would upon the rack of this tough world
> Stretch him out longer."

But there is another aspect of this problem. We must recognise the fact that this request to end suffering by ending life is not always the cry of a spirit stricken past endurance, but rather the dramatic demand of someone whose patience, never too good, is now exhausted. When such a one clamours for an overdose of morphia, I am prone to say, "I would give it to you if I were sure that you would not change your mind half an hour later." Lastly, when the demand to end life is made on behalf of someone else, it is often not the patient but the patient's friends who cannot stand the strain. "Doctor, you must end this agony!" said a woman to me recently, and my reply, "Do you mean yours or your husband's?" brought home to her, if rather sharply, the real position. The inalienable right of another person to live, if he so desires, may be entirely forgotten. "I am sure he does not want to live" may well mean "I do not think I can possibly see him suffering any longer."

LORD HORDER
Medicine and Morals
Lancet, 1934.

Should a Doctor Tell?

It is more difficult to know when to tell in cases of approaching death. I think I should like to know if I had an inoperable cancer or an acute leukæmia, but I don't think this would be true of most people. One gets the "feel" of patients, whether they want the truth or not. Usually it is best to await their approach, and often the form of question helps to determine the answer. One of my best patients and friends—an intelligent, inquisitive, and humorous old man—asked me no single question about his trouble during a long illness with an inoperable bowel cancer. Sometimes the near relatives can help, but usually it has to lie between doctor and patient. A dear old lady of 80 said "Tell me, doctor, I'm not afraid"; and so I told her, and for the many months she lingered on she always had a smile and usually a joke. But for many others the truth would have been mental torture.

And with Pilate one may ask, "What is truth?" At the best we can only tell some of it, for we never know the whole.

PERIPATETIC
Lancet, 1948.

Should a Doctor Tell?

JOHNSON: I deny the lawfulness of telling a lie to a sick man for fear of alarming him. You have no business with consequences: you are to tell the truth. Besides, you are not sure what effect your telling him that he is in danger may have. It may bring his distemper to a crisis, and that may cure him. Of all lying I have the greatest abhorrence of this, because I believe it has been frequently practised on myself.

BOSWELL
Life of Johnson.

Should a Doctor Tell?

I remember an able woman with widespread cancer who said to me, "I wish you had told me first so I could have warned you not to tell my husband. The knowledge does not bother me much, but he cannot take it, and he is rapidly going to pieces." But, as I said to her, the man would soon be knowing it anyway; so why not know it while she was still around to help him face the blow? Often when I see a fine, affectionate husband and wife trying to deceive each other after thirty years in which they have faced together every buffet of fortune, I say, "Why don't you two share this sorrow also? You who have gone through all the great adventures of life hand in hand, surely you should be going through this one, the greatest of all, in the same way. As one of you now starts through the Valley of the Shadow, why shouldn't the other one be staying close? Why shouldn't you both be talking frankly about the future?"

W. C. ALVAREZ
Nervousness, Indigestion and Pain.

Should a Doctor Tell?

Having made your diagnosis, should you communicate it to the patient? Certainly not always, nor in all circumstances. . . . If the prognosis is good, there is no reason why the patient should not know the name of the disease; if bad, a little judicious vagueness of statement is better. The frankness with which most doctors nowadays take patients into their confidence, both as regards diagnosis and treatment, is perhaps to be preferred to the pontifical and mysterious airs so often assumed by our predecessors of another generation, but it is possible to overdo it. It is not every patient who is fit to be told the whole truth about his disease.

Sir ROBERT HUTCHISON
The Principles of Diagnosis
B.M.J., 1928.

[244]

Shall the Doctor Tell ?

Pray Sir how d'ye find your self? says the *Dr.* to his *Patient.*
Why truly, says the *Patient*; I have had a violent sweat.
Oh the best sign in the world quoth the Dr. And then a little
while after he is at it again, with a *Pray how d'ye find your body?*
Alas, says t'other, I have just now such a terrible fit of horror
and shaking upon me! *Why this is all as it should be*, says the
Physician, it shews a mighty strength of nature. And then
he comes over him a third time with the same question again;
why I am all swell'd says t'other, as I had a dropsy; *Best of all*
quoth the *Doctor*, and goes his way. Soon after this comes one
of the sick man's friends to him with the same question, how
he felt himselfe; Why truly so well, says he, that I'm e'en
ready to dye, of I know not how many good signs and
tokens.

Aesop
Fables
Translated by Sir Roger L'Estrange.

We Have our Job to do

Which of you who has a servant out ploughing or looking
after the animals, will say to him when he comes in from the
fields, "Come on now, and sit down at table?" Will not
the master say instead, "Get my supper ready, put on your
apron and wait on me until I have finished eating and drinking; then you can have your supper." Does he thank the
servant for carrying out his orders?

It is just the same with you; when you have done all that
you have been told to, you must say, "We are servants; we
have only done our duty."

St. Luke, xvii. 7-10.
*(Adopting Moffatt's suggestion that the word
"unprofitable" of the Authorised Version is the
addition of some moralising copyist.)*

[245]

The Heart Ennobles any Calling

Rabbi Baroka, a saintly mystic, one day as he was walking through the crowded market-place of his town, met Elijah, the wandering spirit of prophecy in Jewish lore. "Who of all this multitude has the best claim to Heaven?" asks the Rabbi of his spirit companion. The prophet points to a disreputable, weird-looking creature, a turnkey. "That man yonder, because he is considerate to his prisoners, and refrains from all unnecessary cruelty. In that miniature hell over which he presides he has suppressed many a horror." "And who else is here sure of eternal life?" continues the Rabbi. Elijah then points to two motley-dressed fellows, clowns, who were supplying amusement to the bystanders. The Rabbi's astonishment knew no bounds. "Scorn them not," explains the prophet; "it is always their habit, even when not performing for hire, to cheer the depressed and the sorrowful. Whenever they see a sufferer they join him, and by merry talk cause him to forget his grief."

The Talmud.

Death and a Sense of Proportion

The contemplation of death should plant within the soul elevation and peace. Above all it should make us see things in their true light. For all things which seem foolish in the light of death are really foolish in themselves. To be annoyed because So-and-so has slighted us or been somewhat more successful in social distinctions, pulled himself somehow one rung higher up the ladder than ourselves—how ridiculous all this seems when we couple it with the thought of death! To pass each day simply and solely in the eager pursuit of money or of fame, this also seems like living with shadows when one might take one's part with realities. Surely when death is at hand we should desire to say, "I have contributed my grain to the great store of the eternal. I have borne my part in the struggle for goodness." And let no man or woman suppose that the smallest social act of goodness is wasted for society at large. All our help, petty though it be, is needed; and though we know not the manner, the fruit of every faithful service is surely gathered in. Let the true and noble words of a great teacher ring in conclusion upon our ears: "The growing good of the world is partly dependent on unhistoric acts; and that things are not so ill with you and me as they might have been, is half owing to the number who lived faithfully a hidden life and rest in unvisited tombs."

C. G. MONTEFIORE
Aspects of Judaism, 1895.

The Pursuit of Inner Serenity

Socrates speaks:—

"But, O my friend, if this be true, there is great reason to hope that, going whither I go, when I have come to the end of my journey, I shall attain that which has been the pursuit of my life. And therefore I go on my way rejoicing, and not I only, but every other man who believes that his mind has been ready and that he is in a manner purified."

"Certainly," replied Simmias.

"And what is purification but the separation of the soul from the body, as I was saying before; the habit of the soul gathering and collecting herself into herself from all sides out of the body; the dwelling in her own place alone, as in another life, so also in this, as far as she can; the release of the soul from the chains of the body?"

PLATO
Phaedo.

" O Sweet, O Sweet Content "

Let me advise you not to aim too high. The big prizes in our profession are only for the few, and they do not always bring much happiness when gained. "Seekest thou great things? Seek them not," as the wise man said. If you have earned enough for your needs and been able to put a little aside for your old age, and if, at the same time, you have won the esteem of your colleagues and the affection of your patients, you have done well enough, and that measure of success should be within the reach of most of you.

Sir ROBERT HUTCHISON
To match the men, B.M.J., 1941.

" The World is Too Much With Us "

The longer I live, the more I am satisfied of two things: first, that the truest lives are those that are cut rose-diamond fashion, with many facets answering to the many-planed aspects of the world about them; secondly, that society is always trying in some way or other to grind us down to a single flat surface. It is hard work to resist this grinding-down action.

OLIVER WENDELL HOLMES
The Professor at the Breakfast-Table.

Bodily Virtues

Temperance, cleanliness, activity, are the three cardinal virtues of the body, as Faith, Hope and Charity are of the Soul. . . . It is easier to repeat incessant formulae of prayer than persistently to keep one's self unspotted from the world, and it is easier for fat old sinners to paddle about barefoot in the dew at a Kneipp cure than to abandon at once and for ever their little darling sins of greed and indolence.

ANONYMOUS

Covetousness

> "Hast thou found honey? Eat so much as is sufficient
> for thee, lest thou be filled therewith, and vomit
> it. . . ."—Prov. xxv. 16.

He doth not say yet, lest thou bee satisfied; there is no
great feare, nay there is no hope of that, that he will be
satisfied. We know the receipt, the capacity of the ventricle,
the stomach of man, how much it can hold; and wee know
the receipt of all the receptacles of blood, how much blood
the body can have; so wee doe of all the other conduits
and cisterns of the body; But this infinite Hive of honey,
this insatiable whirlpoole of the covetous mind, no Anatomy,
no dissection hath discovered to us. When I looke into the
larders, and cellars, and vaults, into the vessels of our body
for drink, for blood, for urine, they are pottles, and gallons;
when I looke into the furnaces of our spirits, the ventricles of
the heart and of the braine, they are but thimbles; for
spirituall things, the things of the next world, we have no
roome; for temporall things, the things of this, we have no
bounds. How then shall this overeater bee filled with his
honey? So filled, as that he can receive nothing else.

JOHN DONNE
Sermon LXX.

Acceptance

One must not try to escape the pain of life. What do we
suffer for if we lose the knowledge it gives by trying to
evade it?

MAUDE ROYDEN
A Threefold Cord.

Too Many Cares

While nothing disturbs our mental placidity more sadly than straitened means, and the lack of those things after which the Gentiles seek, I would warn you against the trials of the day soon to come to some of you—the day of large and successful practice. Engrossed late and soon in professional cares, getting and spending, you may so lay waste your powers that you may find, too late, with hearts given away, that there is no place in your habit-stricken souls for those gentler influences which make life worth living.

OSLER
Aequanimitas, 1889.

Medicine a Calling

The practice of medicine is an art, not a trade; a calling, not a business; a calling in which your heart will be exercised equally with your head. Often the best part of your work will have nothing to do with potions and powders, but with the exercise of an influence of the strong upon the weak, of the righteous upon the wicked, of the wise upon the foolish. To you, as the trusted family counsellor, the father will come with his anxieties, the mother with her hidden grief, the daughter with her trials, and the son with his follies. Fully one-third of the work you do will be entered in other books than yours. Courage and cheerfulness will not only carry you over the rough places of life, but will enable you to bring comfort and help to the weak-hearted and will console you in the sad hours when, like Uncle Toby, you have "to whistle that you may not weep."

OSLER
The Master-Word in Medicine, 1903.

Sydenham's Choice

I have weighed in a nice and scrupulous balance whether it be better to serve men or to be praised by them, and I prefer the former.

SYDENHAM

The Vocation of Medicine

Whoever applies himself to Medicine should seriously weigh the following considerations: first, that he will one day have to render an account to the Supreme Judge of the lives of sick persons committed to his care. Next, whatever skill or knowledge he may, by the divine favour, become possessed of, should be devoted above all things to the glory of God, and the welfare of the human race. Moreover, let him remember that it is not any base or despicable creature of which he has undertaken the care. For the only-begotten Son of God, by becoming man, recognised the value of the human race, and ennobled by His own dignity the nature He assumed. Finally, the physician should bear in mind that he himself is not exempt from the common lot, but subject to the same laws of mortality and disease as others, and he will care for the sick with more diligence and tenderness if he remembers that he himself is their fellow sufferer.

SYDENHAM
Methodus Curandi Febres, 1666.

This is the Key of the Kingdom

Love will teach us all things: but we must learn how to win love; it is got with difficulty: it is a possession dearly bought with much labour and in long time; for one must love not sometimes only, for a passing moment, but always. There is no man who doth not sometimes love: even the wicked can do that.

And let not men's sin dishearten thee: love a man even in his sin, for that love is a likeness of the divine love, and is the summit of love on earth. Love all God's creation, both the whole and every grain of sand. Love every leaf, every ray of light. Love the animals, love the plants, love each separate thing. If thou love each thing thou wilt perceive the mystery of God in all; and when once thou perceive this, thou wilt thenceforward grow every day to a fuller understanding of it: until thou come at last to love the whole world with a love that will then be all-embracing and universal.

DOSTOEVSKY
The Brothers Karamazov.

VII

AT THE CLOSE OF THE DAY

In the Cool of Day

SOCRATES: Should we not, before going, offer up a prayer to these local deities?

PHAEDRUS: By all means.

SOCRATES: (praying) Beloved Pan, and all ye other gods who haunt this place, grant me beauty in the inward soul, and that the outward and inward may be at one! May I esteem the wise to be the rich; and may I myself have that quantity of gold which a temperate man, and he only, can carry. . . . Anything more? That prayer, I think, is enough for me.

PHAEDRUS: Ask the same for me, Socrates. Friends, methinks, should have all things in common!

SOCRATES: Amen, then. . . . Let us go.

PLATO
Phaedrus.

At the End of the Day

The Sun must not set upon my anger; much less will I let the Sun set upon the anger of God towards me, or sleep in an unrepented sin. Every nights sleep is a *Nunc Dimittis;* then the Lord lets his servant depart in peace. Thy lying down is a valediction, a parting, a taking leave (shall I say so?) a shaking hands with God; and when thou shakest hands with God, let those hands be clean. Enter into thy grave, thy metaphoricall, thy quotidian grave, thy bed, as thou entredst into the Church at first, by Water, by Baptisme; Re-baptise thy self every night, in *Iobs Snow water.* . . . Sleep with cleane hands, either kept cleane all day, by integrity; or washed cleane at night, by repentance.

JOHN DONNE
Sermon XIII.

[255]

A Good Habit

A great teacher of mine, Hughlings Jackson, used to urge upon us the value of sitting down in a comfortable chair at the end of a day's work, allowing one's thoughts to wander around something which had roused one's interest and jotting down the ideas and suggestions to which it would give rise. It *was* a valuable habit; it encouraged independent criticism, it prevented observations from being left isolated, gave them associations, and stimulated one to turn up and explore those byways of thought which are always to be found by those whose minds are fond of rambling.

Sir FARQUHAR BUZZARD
Lancet, 1933.

Advice on Sleep

Whole men of what age or complexion soever they be, should take their natural rest and sleep in the night: and to eschew meridial sleep. But if need should compel a man to sleep after his meat: let him make a pause, and then let him stand and lean and sleep against a cupboard, or else let him sit upright in an chair and sleep. To bedward be you merry or have merry company about you, so that to bedward no anger nor heaviness, sorrow nor pensifulness do trouble or disquiet you. In the night let the windows of your house, especially of your chamber, be closed. When you be in your bed lie a little while on your left side, and sleep on your right side. Let your night cap be of scarlet: and this I do advertise you, to cause to be made a good thick quilt of cotton, or else of pure flocks or of clean wool, and let the covering of it be of white fustian, and lay it on the feather-bed that you do lie on; and in your bed lie not too hot nor too cold, but in a temperance.

Old ancient Doctors of Physic say seven hours of sleep in summer and nine in winter is sufficient for any man; but I do think that sleep ought to be taken as the complexion of man is. When you do rise in the morning, rise with mirth and remember God.

ANDREW BORDE
A Compendious Regyment, 1557.

Drowsy Approaches

But the quincunx of heaven runs low, and 'tis time to close the five ports of knowledge. We are unwilling to spin out our awaking thoughts into the phantasms of sleep, which often continueth precogitations; making cables of cobwebs and wildernesses of handsome groves. Beside Hippocrates hath spoke so little, and the oneirocritical masters have left such frigid interpretations from plants, that there is little encouragement to dream of paradise itself. Nor will the sweetest delight of gardens afford much comfort in sleep; wherein the dulness of that sense shakes hands with delectable odours; and though in the bed of Cleopatra, can hardly with any delight raise up the ghost of a rose.

Night, which Pagan theology could make the daughter of Chaos, affords no advantage to the description of order: although no lower than that mass can we derive its genealogy. All things began in order, so shall they end, and so shall they begin again; according to the Ordainer of order and mystical mathematics of the city of heaven.

Though Somnus in Homer be sent to rouse up Agamemnon, I find no such effects in these drowsy approaches of sleep. To keep our eyes open longer, were but to act our Antipodes. The huntsmen are up in America, and they are already past their first sleep in Persia. But who can be drowsy at that hour which freed us from everlasting sleep? or have slumbering thoughts at that time, when sleep itself must end, and as some conjecture all shall awake again.

SIR THOMAS BROWNE
The Garden of Cyrus.

R

Night Shift

A fine old Bishop lay awake one night worrying his heart out over what seemed to him the evils of a doomed world. As he tossed on his bed at midnight he thought he heard the voice of the Lord saying to him: "Go to sleep now, Bishop. I'll sit up the rest of the night and do the worrying."

Current story.

To Sleep

O soft embalmer of the still midnight!
Shutting with careful fingers and benign
Our gloom-pleased eyes, enbower'd from the light,
Enshaded in forgetfulness divine!
O soothest Sleep! if so it please thee, close,
In midst of this thine hymn, my willing eyes,
Or wait the amen, ere thy poppy throws
Around my bed its lulling charities;
Then save me, or the passed day will shine
Upon my pillow, breeding many woes;
Save me from curious conscience, that still lords
Its strength for darkness, burrowing like a mole;
Turn the key softly in the oiled wards,
And seal the hushed casket of my soul.

JOHN KEATS

Refreshment

There's nothing so refreshin' as sleep, sir, as the servant girl said afore she drank the eggcupful o' laudanum.

DICKENS
Pickwick Papers (Sam Weller).

[258]

This Fleeting World

Grant that we who are fatigued and wearied by the changes of this fleeting world may repose upon Thy eternal changelessness.

The Lord Almighty grant us a quiet night and a perfect end.

From Compline.

Bell-man

From noise of Scare-fires rest ye free,
From Murders—*Benedicite.*
From all mischances, that may fright
Your pleasing slumbers in the night;
Mercie secure ye all, and keep
The Goblin from ye, while ye sleep.
Past one o'clock, and almost two,
My Masters all, *Good day to you!*

ROBERT HERRICK, 1591-1674.

Evening Prayer

Watch Thou, dear Lord, with those who wake, or watch, or weep to-night, and give Thine angels charge over those who sleep. Tend Thy sick ones, O Lord Christ. Rest Thy weary ones. Bless Thy dying ones. Soothe Thy suffering ones. Pity Thine afflicted ones. Shield Thy joyous ones. And all, for Thy Love's sake.

ST. AUGUSTINE, 354-430.

A Day Well Spent

A man should so live that at the close of every day he can repeat: "I have not wasted my day."

The Zohar, circa 1290.

[259]

To Sleep in Peace

Take us, we pray Thee, O Lord of our life, into Thy keeping, this night and for ever. O Thou Light of lights, keep us from inward darkness; grant us so to sleep in peace, that we may arise to work according to Thy will; through Jesus Christ our Lord.

Bishop ANDREWES, 1555-1626.

Before I Lay Me Down to Sleep

Matthew, Mark, Luke and John,
Bless the bed that I lie on.
Before I lay me down to sleep
I give my soul to Christ to keep.
Four corners to my bed,
Four angels there aspread,
Two to foot, and two to head,
And four to carry me when I'm dead.

I go by sea, I go by land,
The Lord made me with his right hand.
If any danger come to me,
Sweet Jesus Christ, deliver me.
He's the branch and I'm the flower,
Pray God send me a happy hour,
And if I die before I wake,
I pray that Christ my soul will take.

Traditional.

Quiet Conscience

Close thine eyes, and sleep secure;
Thy soul is safe, thy body sure.
He that guards thee, he that keeps,
Never slumbers, never sleeps.
A quiet conscience in the breast
Has only peace, has only rest.
The wisest and the mirth of kings
Are out of tune unless she sings:
Then close thine eyes in peace and sleep secure,
No sleep so sweet as thine, no rest so sure.

KING CHARLES I

Guard Us Sleeping

And I will lay me down in peace, and take my rest; for it is Thou, Lord, only, that makest me dwell in safety.

Save us, O Lord, watching, guard us sleeping, that we may watch with Christ, and rest in peace.

From Compline.

VIII

"THIS SANCTUARY OF MY SOUL"

Expectans Expectavi

> This sanctuary of my soul
> Unwitting I keep white and whole,
> Unlatch'd and lit, if Thou should'st care
> To enter or to tarry there.
> With parted lips and outstretch'd hands
> And listening ears Thy servant stands.
> Call Thou early, call Thou late,
> To Thy great service dedicate:
> My soul, keep white and whole.

C. Hamilton Sorley
Marlborough and Other Poems, 1916.

What Made Them Saints?

"Why were the saints saints?" someone asked. And the answer came: "Because they were cheerful when it was difficult to be cheerful, and patient when it was difficult to be patient. They pushed on when they wanted to stand still, and kept silent when they wanted to talk." That was all.

Lord Horder
The Hygiene of a Quiet Mind
Lancet, 1938.

Foundations

Professor—said he, one day,—don't you think your brain will run dry before a year's out, if you don't get the pump to help the cow? Let me tell you what happened to me once. I put a little money in the bank, and bought a check-book, so that I might draw as I wanted, in sums to suit. Things went on nicely for a time; scratching with a pen is as easy as rubbing Aladdin's lamp; and my blank check-book seemed to be a dictionary of possibilities in which I could find all the synonyms of happiness, and realise any one of them on the spot. A check came back to me at last with these two words on it,—*No funds.* My check-book was a volume of waste-paper.

Now, Professor,—said he,—I have drawn something out of your bank, you know, and just so sure as you keep drawing out your soul's currency without making new deposits, the next thing will be, *No funds,*—and then where will you be, my boy?

OLIVER WENDELL HOLMES
The Professor at the Breakfast-Table.

Dr. Shrapnel on Prayer

So in our prayers we dedicate the world to God . . . showing him we know him great in a limitless world, lord of a truth we tend to, have not grasped. I say Prayer is good. I counsel it to you again and again: in joy, in sickness of heart. . . . We make prayer a part of us, praying for no gifts, no interventions; through the faith in prayer opening the soul to the undiscerned. And take this, my Beauchamp, for the good in prayer, that it makes us repose on the unknown with confidence, makes us flexible to change, makes us ready for revolution—for life, then! He who has the fountain of prayer in him will not complain of hazards. Prayer is the recognition of laws; the soul's exercise and source of strength, its thread of conjunction with them. . . . We that fight the living world must have the universal for succour of the truth in it. Cast forth the soul in prayer, you meet the effluence of the outer truth, you join with the creative elements giving breath to you; and that crust of habit which is the soul's tomb; and custom, the soul's tyrant; and pride, our volcano peak that sinks us in a crater; and fear, which plucks the feathers from the wings of the soul and sits it naked and shivering in a vault, where the passing of a common hodman's foot above sounds like the king of terrors coming—you are free of them, you live in the day and for the future, by this exercise and discipline of the soul's faith. Me it keeps young everlastingly. . . .

. . . The true word has its chance of somewhere alighting and striking root. Look not to that. Seeds perish in nature; good men fail. Look to the truth in you, and deliver it, with no afterthought of hope, for hope is dogged by dread; we give our courage as hostage for the fulfilment of what we hope. Meditate on that transaction. Hope is for boys and girls, to whom nature is kind. For men to hope is to tremble. Let prayer—the soul's overflow, the heart's resignation—supplant it.

GEORGE MEREDITH
Beauchamp's Career.

Benediction for Doctors

And I devoutly pray that the blessing of God may attend all your pursuits; rendering them at once subservient to your own felicity, and the good of your fellow-creatures.

Dr. THOMAS PERCIVAL
Medical Ethics, 1803.

The Source of Comfort

St. Paul said:

Blessed be God,
    the Father of mercies,
    and the God of all comfort,
    who comforteth us in all our tribulations;
that we may be able to comfort
    those who are in any trouble,
    with the comfort
    wherewith we ourselves also are comforted of God.

Second Epistle to the Corinthians, i. 3, 4.

[267]

Humility

The man who does good works is more likely to be over-taken by pride in them than by any other moral mischance, and its effect on conduct is injurious in the extreme. Therefore, among the most necessary of virtues is that one which banishes pride; and this is, humility.

> BACHYA IBN PAKUDAH
> Spanish-Jewish philosopher, 11th century.

Delicacy of Feeling

Giving is not the essential thing, but to give with delicacy of feeling. Scripture does not say, "Happy is he who giveth to the poor," but "Happy is he who *wisely considereth* the poor." He who makes the sorrowful rejoice will partake of life everlasting.

> *The Talmud.*

Dedication

God be in my head,
And in my understanding;

God be in mine eyes,
And in my looking;

God be in my mouth,
And in my speaking;

God be in my heart,
And in my thinking;

God be at my end,
And at my departing.

> *Sarum Primer,* 1558.

[268]

Interior Peace

On account of the intimate personal nature of his work, the medical man, perhaps more than any other man, needs that higher education of which Plato speaks,—"that education in virtue from youth upwards, which enables a man eagerly to pursue the ideal perfection." It is not for all, nor can all attain to it, but there is comfort and help in the pursuit, even though the end is never reached. . . . Uncongenial surroundings, an ever-present dissonance between the aspirations within and the actualities without, the oppressive discords of human society, the *lachrymae rerum*, beside the hidden springs of which we sit in sad despair—all these tend to foster in some natures a cynicism quite foreign to our vocation, and to which this inner education offers the best antidote.

OSLER
The Master-Word in Medicine, 1903.

Surprising Judgment

Then shall the King say unto them on his right hand, Come, ye blessed of my Father, inherit the kingdom prepared for you from the foundation of the world: for I was an hungred, and ye gave me meat: I was thirsty, and ye gave me drink: I was a stranger, and ye took me in: naked, and ye clothed me: I was sick, and ye visited me: I was in prison, and ye came unto me.

Then shall the righteous answer him, saying, Lord, when saw we thee an hungred, and fed thee? or thirsty, and gave thee drink? When saw we thee a stranger, and took thee in? or naked, and clothed thee? Or when saw we thee sick, or in prison, and came unto thee?

And the King shall answer and say unto them, Verily I say unto you, Inasmuch as ye have done it unto one of the least of these my brethren, ye have done it unto me.

St. Matthew, xxv. 34-40.

The Glad Heart

Give not over thy soul to sorrow; and afflict not thyself in thine own counsel. Gladness of heart is the life of a man; and the joyfulness of a man is length of days. Love thine own soul, and comfort thy heart: and remove sorrow far from thee; for sorrow hath destroyed many, and there is no profit therein. Envy and wrath shorten a man's days; and care bringeth old age before the time. A cheerful and good heart will have a care of his meat and diet.

Ecclesiasticus.

For Charity

O Lord, who hast taught us that all our doings without charity are nothing worth: Send thy Holy Spirit, and pour into our hearts that most excellent gift of charity, the very bond of peace and of all virtues, without which whosoever liveth is counted dead before thee: Grant this for thine only Son Jesus Christ's sake.

Archbishop CRANMER, 1489-1556
The Collect for Quinquagesima.

Time and Eternity

O God, the protector of all that trust in thee, without whom nothing is strong, nothing is holy; Increase and multiply upon us thy mercy; that, thou being our ruler and guide, we may so pass through things temporal, that we finally lose not the things eternal: Grant this, O heavenly Father, for Jesus Christ's sake our Lord.

The Collect for the Fourth Sunday after Trinity.

New Morning

We give thee hearty thanks, O God, for the rest of the past night and for the gift of a new day with its opportunities of pleasing thee. Grant that we so pass its hours in the perfect freedom of thy service that at eventide we may again give thanks unto thee; through Jesus Christ our Lord.

Daybreak Office of the Eastern Church (3rd century).

Blithe Business

O God, as the day returns and brings us the petty round of irritating duties, help us to perform them with laughter and kind faces; let cheerfulness abound with industry. Give us to go blithely on our business all this day, bring us to our resting beds weary and content and undishonoured, and grant us in the end the gift of sleep.

R. L. STEVENSON

For Understanding

Enlighten our understandings with knowledge of right, and govern our wills by Thy laws, that no deceit may mislead us, no temptation corrupt us; that we may always endeavour to do good and hinder evil. Amidst all the hopes and fears of this world, take not Thy Holy Spirit from us; for the sake of Jesus Christ our Lord.

SAMUEL JOHNSON, 1765.

Light in Darkness

When Adam saw for the first time the sun go down, and an ever-deepening gloom enfold creation, his mind was filled with terror. God then took pity on him, and endowed him with the divine intuition to take two stones—the name of the one was Darkness and the name of the other Shadow of Death—and rub them against each other, and so discover fire. Thereupon Adam exclaimed with grateful joy: "Blessed be the Creator of Light."

The Talmud.

" The Haven Where They Would Be "

Blessed are all Thy saints, our God and King, who have travelled over the tempestuous sea of mortality, and have at last made the desired port of peace and felicity. O, cast a gracious eye upon us who are still in our dangerous voyage. Remember and succour us in our distress, and think on them that lie exposed to the rough storms of troubles and temptations. Strengthen our weakness, that we may do valiantly in this spiritual war; help us against our own negligence and cowardice, and defend us from the treachery of our unfaithful hearts. We are exceeding frail, and indisposed to every virtuous and gallant undertaking. Grant, O Lord, that we may bring our vessel safe to shore, unto our desired haven.

St. Augustine

In the Hand of God

The souls of the righteous are in the hand of God, and no torment shall touch them. They are in peace. Their hope is full of immortality.

Wisdom of Solomon.

For Blessing on Our Work

O God, who hast ordained that whatever is to be desired should be sought by labour, and who by thy blessing bringest honest labour to good effect, invigorate our studies and direct our enquiries, we beseech thee, and let us not linger in ignorance, but enlighten and support us, for the sake of Jesus Christ our Lord.

SAMUEL JOHNSON

Mens Sana in Corpore Sano

Almighty God, bless us, we beseech thee, with healthy bodies, with good understanding, with happy dispositions and with fair habits, and sanctify us throughout, in our bodies, souls and spirits, with the grace of thy Holy Spirit.

JEREMY TAYLOR, 1613-1667.

The Coming of Despair

How can you hope to make the imperfect things perfect, little Timothy, unless you keep before your eyes the vision of God, who is perfection? The prayer that is only against evil destroys itself. If you look at nothing but sorrow and sin, your heart may be at first full of love and pity, but presently anger—righteous perhaps, but still anger—will enter and begin to crowd out love; and then despair will come and deaden pity, and at last will even smother righteous anger. And then there will be silence; for the heart that is filled with despair cannot pray.

FLORENCE CONVERSE
The House of Prayer.

S

[273]

" *Oh, What a Wonderful Morning . . .* "

Bless our coming in and our going out, our thoughts, words and works, and let us begin this day with the praise of the unspeakable sweetness of thy mercy. Hallowed be thy name, thy kingdom come; through Jesus Christ our Lord.

Greek Church Liturgy, third century.

Opportunity

Thank God every morning when you get up that you have something to do which must be done, whether you like it or not. Being forced to work, and forced to do your best, will breed in you temperance, self-control, diligence, strength of will, content, and a hundred other virtues which the idle never know.

CHARLES KINGSLEY

Treasure House

Whatsoever things are true, whatsoever things are honest, whatsoever things are just, whatsoever things are pure, whatsoever things are lovely, whatsoever things are of good report; if there be any virtue, and if there be any praise, think on these things.

St. Paul's letter to the Philippians, iv. 8.

For Patience

O Lord, move us by Thine example to show kindness and do good. Grant us such patience and forbearance with all sufferers, gracious or ungracious, grateful or ungrateful, that in our stumbling walk and scant measure, they may yet discern a vestige of Thee, and give Thee the glory.

CHRISTINA G. ROSSETTI

A Meditation

O Lord, it is the business of a perfect man never to withdraw his mind from attentive thought of heavenly things, and thus to pass amidst many cares without care; not as one destitute of all feeling, but, by the privilege of a free mind, cleaving to no creature with inordinate affection. . . . Behold! meat, drink, clothing, and other necessaries for the support of the body, are burdensome to a fervent spirit. Grant to me such refreshments moderately, and not to be entangled with an undue desire of them.

THOMAS À KEMPIS

For Sympathy

Give me, O Thou Father of Compassions, such a tenderness and meltingness of Heart that I may be deeply affected with all the Miseries and Calamities outward or inward of my Brethren, and diligently keep them in Love; Grant that I may not only seek my own things, but also the things of others. O that this mind may be in us all, which was in the Lord Jesus, that we may love as Brethren, be Pitiful and Courteous, and endeavour heartily and vigorously to keep the Unity of the Spirit in the Bond of Peace, and the God of Pity, Mercy and Peace be with us all.

THOMAS À KEMPIS

A Plant called Reverence

I have in the corner of my heart a plant called Reverence,
which I find needs watering at least once a week.

OLIVER WENDELL HOLMES

Under a Wiltshire Apple Tree

Some folks as can afford,
So I've heard say,
Set up a sort of cross
Right in the garden way
To mind 'em of the Lord.
But I, when I do see
Thik apple tree
An' stoopin' limb
All spread wi' moss,
I think of Him
And how He talks wi' me.

I think of God
And how He trod
That garden long ago;
He walked, I reckon, to and fro
And then sat down
Upon the groun'
Or some low limb
What suited Him,
Such as you see
On many a tree,
And on thik very one
Where I at set o' sun
Do sit and talk wi' He.

And, mornings, too, I rise and come
An' sit down where the branch be low;
A bird do sing, a bee do hum,
The flowers in the border blow,
And all my heart's so glad and clear
As pools be when the sun do peer,
As pools a-laughing in the light
When mornin' air is swep' an' bright,
As pools what got all Heaven in sight,
So's my heart's cheer
When He be near.

He never pushed the garden door,
He left no footmark on the floor;
I never heard 'Un stir nor tread
And yet His Hand do bless my head,
And when 'tis time for work to start
I takes Him with me in my heart.
And when I die, pray God I see
At very last thik apple tree
An' stoopin' limb,
And think of Him
And all He been to me.

ANNA BUNSTON DE BARY
Collected Poems.

Safe Lodging

May he support us all the day long, till the shades lengthen,
and the evening comes, and the busy world is hushed, and
the fever of life is over, and our work is done. Then in His
mercy may He give us a safe lodging, and a holy rest, and
peace at the last.

CARDINAL NEWMAN
A Sermon on Wisdom and Innocence, 1843.

The Arrow

In the forest of the air,
Jesus, with his quiver bare,
came upon a sturdy tree,
lopt a branch, and it was me.

At one end he fix'd a head
barb'd, and dipt in venom red,
venom that could raise the dead,
life-blood for my Safety shed.

Then he split the arrow through,
gave it speed with feathers two;
nick'd and finish'd, I was stor'd
in the quiver of the Lord.

Presently he spied the foe,
strung me ready in his bow;
still I fly, and still I fly,
flying till the day I die:

Speed he gave me, and good aim;
may I, in my Maker's name,
never use it to his shame,
never from the purpose slip

Of his master-marksmanship,
never, never cease to try,
that if the arrow fall awry
none may blame his Archery.

CHRISTOPHER HASSALL
Poems.

[278]

Mediators

Christ has no body now on earth but yours, no hands but yours, no feet but yours; yours are the eyes through which is to look out Christ's compassion to the world, yours are the feet with which He is to go about doing good, and yours are the hands with which he is to bless us now.

STE. TERESA

For Amiableness

O Thou Who art infinitely delightful to the sons of men, make me and the sons of men infinitely delightful unto Thee. Replenish our actions with amiableness and beauty; that as Thou in all Thy works are pleasing to us, we in all our works may be so to Thee.

THOMAS TRAHERNE, 1620-1674.

"Safe where all Safety's Lost"

That a man has a restful and peaceful life in God is good. That a man endures a painful life in patience, that is better; but that a man has his rest in the midst of a painful life, that is best of all.

MEISTER ECKHART, 1260-1327.

Easy Burden

The Redeemer of mankind, whose words never could deceive, said that His yoke was easy and His burden light, and according to that He could prescribe nothing to our practice which was impossible to be done.

DON QUIXOTE

Fellow Workers

O Lord, help me to understand that you ain't going to let nothing come my way that you and me together can't handle.

Negro prayer.

De Minimis

As for me, my bed is made. I am done with great things and big things, great organisations and big successes. And I am for those tiny, invisible, molecular forces which work from individual to individual, creeping in through the crannies of the world like so many soft rootlets, or like the capillary oozing of water, but which, if you give them time, will rend the hardest monuments of man's pride.

WILLIAM JAMES

An Old Gaelic House Motto

> May God bless the dwelling:
> Each stone and beam and stave,
> All food and drink and clothing:
> May health of man be always there.

Traditional.

For the Guest-room

The pilgrim they laid in a large upper chamber whose window opened towards the sun-rising; the name of the chamber was Peace.

Traditional.

The Conclusion

> Even such is Time, that takes in trust
>   Our youth, our joys, our all we have,
> And pays us but with earth and dust;
>   Who in the dark and silent grave,
> When we have wandered all our ways,
> Shuts up the story of our days;
> But from this earth, this grave, this dust,
> My God shall raise me up, I trust.

> Sir WALTER RALEGH, 1618
> *Written the night before his execution; found in his Bible in the Gate-house at Westminster.*

INDEX

[281]

Printed at Arcata Graphics/Kingsport

Gomers

The Dean was a gentle, bearded man, a pipe-smoking neurologist. He loved to sail in the San Juan islands. He was a far-seeing person and was not given to anger. The failures, large and small, of his medical students were duly noted, but the Dean always saw past these failures to the future successes of his embryo physicians. The only times I ever saw the Dean angry was when he heard someone using the term "gomer."

Many say that this term is an acronym for "Get out of my emergency room!" a phrase frequently yelled at gomers by emergency room physicians. The gomers themselves were down-and-outers. They were the alcoholics, the addicts, and the senile, raging geriatrics. The term was ubiquitous among the students and house staff at the hospitals in our university system. Underground pamphlets circulated that described the classification of gomers, competitions of legendary gomers, and even gomer olympics. Elaborate point systems were invented to differentiate the ordinary gomer from the supergomer, the title supergomer being awarded for accumulating 150 gomer points. Making ward rounds on these devastated human beings was always turbulent. Gomers always had every possible complication, and treating them was terribly frustrating.

The house staff was surprised at the vehemence with which the Dean attacked the term gomer but was not deterred in its use. We intimated among ourselves that the Dean was obviously far removed from clinical medicine and had forgotten what things were like on the wards.

On the pediatric service a few years later, I supervised the care of a 3-year-old boy named Allan who was dying of hepatic failure. The medical details are not relevant, but it would be difficult to imagine a more depressing case. Bleeding complications rather than hepatic coma threatened to become the terminal event, and the child was in pain.

I noticed that the house staff always became paradoxically whimsical as we discussed Allan's case. They indulged in what I considered to be medical fantasy, that is, going off on tangents related to remote and horrendous complications. There was a great deal of inappropriate levity and hilarity. I knew that it was not malicious; individually they were as upset about the illness and their inability to affect it as I was. It reminded me of the way we had talked about gomers, and that disturbed me.

One particularly grim day we made rounds on Allan the morning after his most serious hemorrhage. His parents had finally gone home to rest, and he was sitting alone on his hospital bed. As we were leaving the room he suddenly asked, "Will you read to me for a few whiles?"

Our silence was deafening, and the looks of sheer panic on the faces of my colleagues surprised me. Suddenly I realized that all of the inappropriate hilarity, the medical fantasy, and the talk of gomers was a defense against the terrible fear of failure and death. I realized how I, too, had hidden behind the jesting, cynical demeanor and brusque, busy professionalism. At that moment I saw the callow inexperience clearly revealed in myself and in my colleagues by all those years of gomer talk.

We read *The Cat in the Hat* twice, followed by *The Golden Book of Dinosaurs*, and were about a third of the way into *Selected Mother Goose* when my little patient fell asleep.

Singing cricket drawn by Dr R. D. Alexander, Museum of Zoology, University of Michigan, Ann Arbor.

JIMINY

"On the other side of my own life as a sick man, I want to tell you what I do with my time. As Dr. Posner said, I do write; I do lecture; I do read and dedicate my own life to those great issues which have dominated it for so many decades. I believe I can still be useful in a number of ways . . . In short, life does not stop with terminal illness—only the patient stops when he doesn't have the will to go forward with life until death overtakes him. That happens to everybody. So I end with two thoughts. One, you could be great inspirers of that idea and can prolong what is truly life by your inspiration—that a patient continue work and interest as the greatest therapy of all. Second, you can forget all about terminal illness—everybody is terminal. I think that, too, is a great message which can perpetuate for your patients and their families what is really worthwhile in life, and that is the excitement and the expectation of living the days that you are given to live. . . ."

JACOB K. JAVITS (1904–1986)
U.S. Senator
(New York, Republican)

"That's insubordination!" he said. "You're supposed to be working for me."

"No, I'm not," I said. "I'm not working for you. I never in my life worked for anybody but a patient."

> PAUL B. MAGNUSON, M.D., upon being
> fired as Chief Medical Director by
> Carl Gray, Administrator of the
> U.S. Veterans Administration
>
> MAGNUSON, PB: *Ring the Night Bell:
> The Autobiography of a Surgeon.*
> Boston, MA: Little, Brown and
> Company, 1960, p. 344

"Without scientific knowledge, a compassionate wish to serve mankind's health is meaningless, and it should be possible to acknowledge the triumphs of medicine without denigrating the art."

HERRMAN L. BLUMGART, M.D. (1895–1977)
Internist, Boston, Massachusetts